THE AMERICAN JEWISH COMMUNITY

Program in Judaic Studies
Brown University
BROWN STUDIES ON
JEWS AND THEIR SOCIETIES
Edited by
Jacob Neusner
Wendell S. Dietrich, Ernest S. Frerichs,
Calvin Goldscheider, Alan Zuckerman

This volume is published in cooperation with

The Israel-Diaspora Institute

Tel Aviv University, Ramat Aviv, 69978
Tel Aviv, ISRAEL

Number 3
THE AMERICAN JEWISH COMMUNITY
Social Science Research and
Policy Implications

by

Calvin Goldscheider

THE AMERICAN JEWISH COMMUNITY: SOCIAL SCIENCE RESEARCH AND POLICY IMPLICATIONS

by

CALVIN GOLDSCHEIDER

with comments by

Reuven Hammer
Rita E. Hauser
Harold S. Himmelfarb
Richard G. Hirsch
Wolfe Kelman
Deborah Dash Moore
Bernard Reisman
Jonathan D. Sarna
Alexander Schindler
Charles E. Silberman
Ira Silverman
Jacob B. Ukeles

Scholars Press

Atlanta, Georgia

THE AMERICAN JEWISH COMMUNITY

Social Science Research and
Policy Implications
by

Calvin Goldscheider

© 1986
Brown University

Library of Congress Cataloging in Publication Data

Goldscheider, Calvin.
    The American Jewish community.

    (Brown studies on Jews and their societies ; no. 3)
    1. Jews--United States--Social conditions. 2. Jews--United States--
Cultural assimilation. 3. United States--Social conditions--1980-
I. Title. II. Series.
E184.J5G6264   1986   305.8'924'073   86-26051
ISBN 1-55540-081-7 (alk. paper)
ISBN 1-55540-082-5 (pbk. : alk. paper)

Printed in the United States of America
on acid-free paper

TO

my brother, Harvey

and

my sister, Ethel

They exemplify by their lives, their families, and their commitments, creative American Jewish responses to the challenges of Judaism and Jewishness.

CONTENTS

PREFACE

The core essay in this volume presents a sociological overview of the American Jewish community in the 1980s in the context of where it has been and where it is heading. It challenges some of the accepted wisdom about the assimilation of American Jews, arguing for a reassessment of the ways in which patterns of social change have been interpreted in the past. But the issues addressed are not primarily theoretical, abstract, or solely of analytic concern to social scientists. The key concern is how the accepted wisdom may have misdirected our understanding of the American Jewish community and how a different interpretation would generate new policies to reshape the ways in which the Jewish commitments of American Jews may be enhanced.

Two critical questions are addressed: Are Jews different from non-Jews? And if so, what do these differences mean for group assimilation and continuity? The focus is on the major features of American Jewish life--marriage and the family and therefore the links between the generations; residence and migration, where Jews live and therefore their connections to Jewish communities; social class, lifestyle, education, and therefore the resources available and the group networks that are the basis of communal life; and the religious, communal affiliations, ethnic identification, and behavior of American Jews to know the cultural and organizational setting of the Jewish community, the arenas of intense Jewish interaction with other Jews, and the quality of Jewish life.

I review what social science has learned about American Jews and their communities and the emerging patterns in the 1980s. I focus on the patterns among Jews who are part of the core (or cores) of the Jewish community as well as those on the margins, about Jewish families, children and the changing roles of American Jewish women, and on the ethnic and religious quality of Jewish life in America. My conclusions, based on new research findings and a systematic interpretation of these findings, are that generational changes are best understood and interpreted in the context of the development of new bases of group continuity that are emerging in the United States in the 1980s. The major transformations of the American Jewish community over the last century, from the eastern European foreign born toward the fifth generation in America, has resulted in a different community than in the past. The community is stronger in some ways and weaker in others but, on the whole, continues to be characterized by multiple bases of cohesion. It is inconsistent with the evidence available to treat these changes among American Jews in the context of the assimilation of American Jews to American society. Consequently, policies need to be directed to the major strengths of the community, to build on the sources of cohesion already evident in the community, and not presume the continued deterioration and decline of the American Jewish community. Policies should be based on the continuous monitoring of social changes characterizing the community and on an evaluation of programs and policies that enhance the multiple ways Jews express religious and ethnic dimensions of Jewishness in America.

The second part of the essay deals directly with the policy implications of this new social scientific evidence and assessment. Building on the interpretation of cohesion and strength of the American Jewish community, I tried to specify the goals and arenas of policy for a voluntaristic community in a pluralistic society. I show the importance of reexamining issues of Jewish family life, Jewish education, demography, and the critical linkages between Israel and the American Jewish community.

Emerging from these are three illustrative policy recommendations. These include (1) a summer program for unaffiliated or marginal Jewish teenagers, (2) support for modern Jewish studies on the college campuses, and (3) the need to reorient the changing relationships between the Jewish leadership in Israel and the United States.

The essay was sent to social scientists, Rabbis, historians, and Jewish communal leaders, with the hope that some would respond, disagree, or debate the issues and present alternatives from their perspectives. The focus was specifically on the policy connections, since the general social science argument would be debated in other, more appropriate, forums. Twelve communal leaders and scholars responded in writing and these are presented with but minor editorial changes in the second part of this volume. In response to their written comments, I prepared a brief epilogue to clarify my original arguments. I incorporated in my response reactions I received to these ideas from a much broader range of verbal communications, discussions, and debates that I have had over the past several years as I have researched and thought through the issues.

The impetus for preparing the original essay was the urging of my dear friend and former student at the University of California, Berkeley, Shelly Schreter. Shelly has tried over the years to convince me of the value of translating my sociological and demographic research into practical policy concerns for Jewish communal leaders and to address the issues confronting the future of the American Jewish community. After much urging, I plunged into the challenge only to discover how very difficult is such an undertaking and yet how important it is to bridge the gap between the worlds of social science scholarship and Jewish communal policy. There are few guidelines available. Shelly helped by trying to keep me on course, by raising new questions and suggesting new avenues of policy consideration, by reading and rereading drafts of my essay, sparing no red ink to correct my mistakes and force me to clarify my ambiguities. Only friends who understand the issues and share common goals can work in that way. As a result, I am indebted to him as I have learned much from him. The essay is clearer and sharper because of his efforts. The volume exists because of his vision and dedication to get things done. He prepared a brief Afterword that concludes the book.

I have taught courses and seminars incorporating these materials at the Hebrew University, Brandeis University, and Brown University. Again, I have learned much from my students. I owe a special debt of gratitude to those colleagues and friends who took time out to comment, often in great detail, on the original drafts of the essay. Those who responded in writing and are included in this volume were most gracious. I am grateful for their supportive as well as their critical comments.

I have presented some of these ideas in previous publications, particularly in *Jewish Continuity and Change: Emerging Patterns in America,* published in 1986 by Indiana University Press, based on research completed in the fall of 1982 when I finished a two year period as visiting Professor of Contemporary Jewish Studies at Brandeis University and was affiliated with their Center for Modern Jewish Studies. Parts of the basic argument have been presented at conferences and lectures in Israel and in the United States. An early and briefer version was presented in June, 1984 at the Hebrew University conference on Jewish education in Jerusalem and in September, 1984 in Chicago at an academic Conference sponsored by the American Friends of the Hebrew University. Parts have been included in an essay I prepared as the 25th anniversary commemorative lecture for the Bernard Horwich Jewish Community Center in Chicago and in lectures I have presented at Boston Hebrew College, Brandeis University, and at the Shearith Israel, the Sephardic and Portuguese Congregation in Montreal, Canada. The detailed essay was presented for discussion at a special meeting held in Jerusalem in conjunction with the Ninth World Congress of Jewish Studies, August, 1985, organized by the Israel-Diaspora Institute and coordinated by Shelly Schreter. About 20 social scientists and Jewish communal leaders from the United States and Israel attended and discussed the issues raised by the essay. Their reactions forced me again to clarify my position.

These occasions and the responses of colleagues and friends have been helpful in clarifying my ideas. In particular, I want to thank Sidney Goldstein, Sergio DellaPergola, Shelly Schreter, Tzvi Abusch, Steven M. Cohen, Rabbi Howard Joseph, Norma Joseph, Larry Sternberg, as well as those who responded in writing.

As in all my work on contemporary Jews and their communities, I am indebted to Jacob Neusner and Alan Zuckerman, Brown University, colleagues and friends, who make me work hard to defend my ideas and sharpen my arguments. They have made Judaic Studies at Brown University a nurturing environment for research and teaching about Jews; no one could expect to have more supportive or stimulating colleagues. For continual support of my research I also want to thank the director of the Program in Judaic Studies, Professor Ernest Frerichs, and the Dean of the Faculty, John Quinn. Part of the processing costs of preparing this volume for publication was provided by Brown University Faculty Development Fund and the resources of the Program in Judaic Studies. Other funds were provided by the Israel-Diaspora Institute in Tel Aviv, Israel, which initiated the project as a whole and providèd financial support for the preparation of this publication. This volume is therefore a joint undertaking of the Program in Judaic Studies of Brown University and the Israel-Diaspora Institute of Tel Aviv. None of these institutions bears responsibility for the interpretation and presentation of the materials in this volume. Carol Walker typed several drafts of the manuscript and prepared it in final form for publication. I am most grateful to her for her skill, patience, and cheerfulness.

My work in sociology and demography, in general, and on contemporary Jews, in particular, relies continually on the helpful insights and high scholarly standards of Frances Kobrin Goldscheider, Chair of the Department of Sociology of Brown University. She has read and listened to the arguments presented here more times than is reasonable to ask of anyone. She has always responded with encouragement and support as well as with great care, patience, and constructive criticism. She has spared me from making errors of fact and of judgment and continues to reshape my thinking. Her own research in American family and ethnic patterns addresses issues in the forefront of sociology and demography and has had a major impact on my research. She is truly a partner in everything I do.

I shared an earlier draft of my essay with my brother, Rabbi Harvey L. Goldscheider. He is a Rabbi and teacher, who in the course of our lives has taught me a great deal about Jews, Judaism, and the American Jewish community. He disagreed with much of the thrust of the essay. He provided me with a detailed written critique and in extensive discussions he suggested areas where my essay was limited as a basis for understanding the American Jewish community. He forced me more than anyone to clarify where I stand and what the issues are as I see them.

I also discussed the themes of my essay with my sister, Ethel Fischer, in Jerusalem and in Baltimore. She too is an educator, active professionally in the teaching of Judaism and involved in the organization and administration of Jewish education. She is aware of the strengths and limitations of American Jewish life and has worked hard to convey to the next generation the values of

Jewishness.

I dedicate this volume to my brother and sister, in love and respect, and in the hope that our disagreements over interpretations do not obscure the much larger areas of shared perspective and commitments to living Jewishly in our communities.

Calvin Goldscheider
July, 1986
Sivan, 5746

THE ISRAEL-DIASPORA INSTITUTE (IDI)

The IDI is a policy-planning research body with an action orientation devoted to studying the dynamics and problematics of Israel-Diaspora relations in their main dimensions, and to providing concrete policy recommendations for their reinforcement and enhancement. It also provides a forum for airing new ideas on current Israel-Diaspora issues and for developing new models of Israel-Diaspora relations based on the principles of direct and personalized peer interaction and partnership in decision-making. It operates from offices on the campus of Tel Aviv University.

The IDI was founded in 1981 by a group of senior communal leaders and academics from Israel and the Diaspora, who shared a consensus on several key points: The critical importance of Israel-Diaspora relations as a major facet of contemporary Jewish life; the need for a "think tank" to monitor and interpret the changes in the Jewish world, and to bring the best available minds to bear in coping practically with the central issues on the world Jewish agenda; and the necessity for making such a body an effective instrument for Jewish unity, through its being a genuinely joint Israel-Diaspora endeavor in every aspect of its activity.

The IDI has worked extensively on Israel-Diaspora economic cooperation, and has a special division named in memory of the late Jacob Levinson, which concentrates on this sphere. Considerable effort has also been invested in a series of studies in the field of Jewish education. Other topics on which the IDI has been (or is now) active include: The impact of Project Renewal on

Israel-Diaspora relations; the input of American Jewry into U.S. foreign policy in the Middle East; the policy implications of research findings on contemporary American Jewry; the determinants of Soviet policies toward Soviet Jewry; and more.

The IDI has a division devoted to fostering the relations between French-speaking Jewry and Israel, through cultural, intellectual and youth exchanges; translations, newsletters and other publications; and other activities.

In addition, the IDI serves as a catalyst or facilitator in initiating important developments in Israel-Diaspora relations, e.g. its consultancy role with the World Assembly of Young Jewish Leadership (also known as the "Moriah" process) and its convening of an international colloquium on the "Who is a Jew?" issue, in the context of the dangers to Jewish unity in our time.

Finally, the IDI works on building new models of Israel-Diaspora relations based on the partnership and peer interaction principles cited earlier, and on the corollary of Israel-Diaspora interdependence, i.e., active mutual involvement in contending with pressing, current problems. The IDI was thus involved in setting up joint projects linking the Jewish community federations of Los Angeles and San Francisco with the Tel Aviv Municipality; and is now working with joint Israel-Diaspora teams on issues connected with extremism and democracy in Israel.

PART ONE

THE AMERICAN JEWISH COMMUNITY:
SOCIAL SCIENCE RESEARCH AND
POLICY IMPLICATIONS

Calvin Goldscheider

1

Outline

I.   Introduction

II. A Sociological Overview of the American Jewish Community

      The Assimilation Perspective
      Ethnicity and the Cohesion of the American Jewish
          Community
      Jewish Cohesion and the Marginals
      Family and Generational Continuity
      Quality of Jewish Life

III. Policy Perspectives

      Policy Orientations, Targets, and Goals
      Arenas for Policy Development
      Three Policy Recommendations

      A. Summer Program for Unaffiliated Teenagers
      B. Modern Jewish Studies
      C. Leadership Issues in Israel and America

I. INTRODUCTION

This paper is divided into two major sections. The first is a concise and focused overview of the sociology and demography of the American Jewish community. In large part it is based on two books of mine which have recently been published: (1) *The Transformation of the Jews*, University of Chicago Press, 1984 (with Alan Zuckerman) is a comparative-historical analysis of Jewish life in Europe, Israel, and America in the last century. We address the questions, how have the processes of modernization affected the social, economic, cultural, and political life of Jews and their communities? Has modernization led to the assimilation of Jews? (2) *Jewish Continuity and Change: Emerging Patterns in America*, Indiana University Press, 1986, is a detailed socio-demographic analysis of family, population, and stratification patterns in an American Jewish community. The empirical basis of the patterns discussed in this paper is documented in that volume. I review here the highlights of the evidence, some of which is controversial. The statistical analysis is presented systematically and with documentation in both volumes. The summary provided here focuses on policy-related issues. I ask the reader to be sceptical and critical of the evidence and the interpretation, as well as responsive to the policy issues. Those who want to study the detailed evidence are invited to examine these volumes.

Building on a review of these analyses, a second part of this paper outlines a series of policy orientations and issues. Several specific policy recommendations are developed which reflect the theoretical and empirical conclusions of recent social science research.

5

It is the premise of this paper that the specification of policies for a community requires fundamental knowledge about its population, social and economic resources, political and institutional organization, its cultural life, attitudes and values. No brief essay can cover all of these areas of communal life or attempt to address the heterogeneity among Jewish communities. Nevertheless there are several basic processes which are critical to the understanding of the dynamics of the American Jewish community. These emerge out of recent social scientific research and provide the foundation for policy reformulation.

All policies, as all analyses, have implicit theoretical assumptions about the community, its boundaries and characteristics, and the impact of broader social changes on the strength and solidarity of its constituency. Much of the evidence and its interpretation have specific policy relevance. We attempt to bridge the gap between research and policy, recognizing both the limitations of research and the constraints on policy implementation.

II. A SOCIOLOGICAL OVERVIEW OF THE AMERICAN JEWISH COMMUNITY

The Assimilation Perspective

There is a deep-rooted feeling among many Jews and some Jewish professionals in the United States and in Israel that there is no future in the long run for the American Jewish community. While the precise length of the long run is a matter of ambiguity and disagreement, there seems to be some consensus that American Jewry is progressively weakening. It is shrinking in size, diminishing in numbers in local areas and nationally. The quality of Jewish life is weakening as well. American Jews are (and have been over the last several generations) assimilating into the general culture and society. This argument is bolstered by selected empirical evidence, theoretical considerations, and ideological commitments.

It has been reported that intermarriage between Jews and non-Jews is increasing, threatening American Jewish continuity. Young Jews are not having children and fertility rates are below population replacement. Synagogues and Temples are empty except for a few times a year and traditional ritual observances such as Kashrut and Shabbat are maintained by an isolated few. Young Jews leave the parental home to attend colleges and universities where contacts with non-Jews and secular-Christian values result in their alienation from Judaism and the Jewish community. They no longer enter the businesses of their fathers; in their occupational achievements and new professions they have severed their ties with family and other Jews. Men and women of the younger generation have been liberated from their family and community as well as from the traditional values which, in the

7

past, were central to Jewish communal continuity. By moving to new locations and adopting new life styles, they move away from the institutions and organizations established by the Jewish community. The educational attainments and occupational career orientations of the younger generation of Jewish women have resulted in the development of life styles not conducive to marriage, childbearing, or familism.

In sum, this approach seems to suggest a consistent portrait of generational assimilation. The American Jewish community is therefore by its assimilation becoming fewer in number and of diminished quality. Demographically and Jewishly, the Jewish community appears to be moving in the direction of extinction. If the end is not quite in sight, it is at least around the corner.

This somewhat oversimplified doomsday prophecy fits neatly into a world view, an ideological position and theoretical framework, which is common in the social sciences and popular among selected Jewish philosophers and ideologists.

There has been a general theme in the social sciences that becoming modern means losing those particular qualities which distinguish and mark people off from one another. Thus, for example, in the transition from traditional to modern society, racial differences are expected to diminish; social differences due to gender are assumed to decline. More and more people are expected to be judged on the basis of merit and individual achievement rather than by family background, group status, and inherited traits. ("Yichus" is not expected to count in the modern world.)

In this analysis, social scientists have predicted the declining salience of religion and ethnicity. Religion and ethnicity, so they have argued, are legacies of the past. They are traditional and tribal. The particularism of ethnicity and religion has no place in the universalism associated with modernity. In the urban-metropolitan setting of modern society, being ethnic or religious is associated with traditional not modern; it is part of the past not of the future. In this theoretical mode of thought, ethnicity and religiosity are at best cultural nostalgia and psychological anchors of identity. They are as "cute" as gefilte fish and cholent made in a gourmet style but also equally irrelevant in the lives of people and their values. This contrasts sharply with the centrality and depth of Jewishness and Judaism in some distant past in the lives of grandparents or great-grandparents. Ethnicity and religion have become marginal to the daily round of activities of modern Jewish men and women.

This social science theory of the assimilation of ethnic-religious groups in modern society has been drawn on by a variety of philosophical and ideological positions. One dominant stream is a particularly interesting version of the theory of Zionism and Jewish peoplehood. This ideology sees the eventual demise of Jewish communities outside of the Jewish state. The future of Jews in the diaspora, so the ideology argues, is doomed by the enemies of the Jews or by their own assimilation. Anti-semitism, discrimination, and holocaust await diaspora Jews -- it is the overriding fact of Jewish history. And if the non-Jews and the power of a racial state do not succeed in erasing diaspora Jewish communities, then the power of assimilation will integrate, absorb, and eradicate those unique traditional features of Jewish life. When opportunities emerge for Jews to participate fully in the modern world, they assimilate, lose their Jewishness, run after the "Golden Calf" of modernity.

Taking together the strength of the prevailing consensus, the consistency of the theory, and the salience of the ideology, one major conclusion has been reached: the American Jewish community as the most modern diaspora community, confronted with social and economic opportunities, and an open, pluralist, multi-ethnic, racial and religious, and tolerant society, is assimilating. Jews are losing their Jewishness and their religious uniqueness. They are diminishing quantitatively and qualitatively through increasing levels of intermarriage, high rates of non-marriage, and childlessness, through secularization, educational attainments, occupational achievement and through social contacts and moving away from traditional Jewish neighborhoods.

Ethnicity and the Cohesion of the American Jewish Community

Recent social scientific evidence on American Jews and other white ethnics and the continuing salience of religion and ethnicity in modern American society have challenged these conclusions. Alternative interpretations of the emerging patterns of ethnicity in America point to the need to reconsider the fundamental assumptions of the assimilation perspective. The argument which forms the basis of this paper takes the view exactly opposite to the thrust of the assimilation-disappearance position. Stated boldly

9

and simply, the argument is that the American Jewish community is a powerful and cohesive community. It has strong anchors of social, religious and family life; it is neither diminishing demographically nor weakening Jewishly. It is not about to disappear nor is it moving in the direction of disappearance. It is growing in a variety of ways, becoming more Jewish, stronger, more articulate, more cohesive as a community over the last several generations. In short, the American Jewish community has been transformed. It has dramatically changed from what it was 20-40 or 60 years ago. In the process of this transformation it has become stronger, not weaker. If we choose to describe what has happened over the last half century in America as assimilation, then assimilation has led to stronger ethnic group cohesion. It is much more appropriate to describe the potential future of the American Jewish community as one entering a period of flourishing and creative development than one reflecting the final gasps of a declining, weakening, struggling to survive remnant.

This thesis is not based on an ideological commitment; it is not an outgrowth of a theological or religious position. It is based on new, detailed social scientific evidence and a reanalysis of historical and comparative materials on Jews and other ethnic groups in the United States and elsewhere. This paper reviews that evidence briefly, outlining some of the revised analyses and suggesting policy orientations and guidelines which flow from these data.

Fundamentally, the argument is that modernization does not lead to the total absorption of ethnic and religious groups but often, particularly in pluralistic societies, *creates* new bases of cohesion for them. More importantly, modernization transforms ethnic and religious groups and shapes their communities in new ways. The changes associated with group transformation have often been misinterpreted as assimilation. Change, as we shall illustrate below, does not necessarily mean ethnic or religious group disappearance and does not necessarily imply the weakening of ethnic and religious communities.

The argument is not simply a question of semantics. It is not only an issue of theory. It is not the rejection of one ideological position, replacing it with another ideology. It is not simply a question of the glass being half-full or half-empty. It is not an interpretation of optimism versus pessimism. It is an

10

interpretation of new social scientific evidence about ethnic cohesion, which has led to a revision of older theories. It is an argument that develops a new theory or perspective which incorporates the evidence and has implications for new policy directions for the Jewish community.

Since we base our argument on social science evidence, we need to provide an outline of our research findings. We start with the examination of Jews in their communities, rather than as individuals, and focus on the key features of Jewish communal life:

*marriage and family formation and, hence, the links between generations;

*residence and migration to establish where people live and their links to communities;

*social class, life style, education, and jobs to know what resources Jews have and how these are related to group networks;

*religion and communal affiliations, identification and behavior to identify the cultural content of Jewishness and the institutional and organizational settings where Jews interact with other Jews.

We ask two interrelated questions about these aspects of social life:

(1) Are Jews different from others? If so,

(2) What do these differences mean for group assimilation or group continuity?

These two questions are separated since changes in group distinctiveness do not automatically or necessarily imply assimilation. There is a widespread assumption, explicit in social science and implicit in policy, that ethnic change necessarily leads to a decline in group cohesion. Residential integration, secularization, increasing educational levels, occupational mobility, family size reduction, and intermarriage are often assumed to mean declines in the salience of ethnicity. In particular, these processes have been understood as implying decreases in

11

interaction among ethnics. That set of assumptions is our core research question, rather than a logical conclusion derived from the changing distinctiveness of groups.

To ask about the distinctiveness of Jews we need to compare Jews and non-Jews over time. Moreover, we need to disentangle the sources of distinctiveness to evaluate the question of continuities. It is critical to know, for example, whether the sources of distinctiveness are temporary and transitory or whether they are embedded in the social structure. Often the analysis of Jews is limited to descriptions without comparisons. When comparisons are made, they tend to be between current patterns and an idealized, nostalgic past. When Jews and non-Jews are compared, elementary methodological cautions are often ignored, such that Jews (who in the United States are located in select large metropolitan areas, engaged in particular jobs, with particular educational backgrounds) are compared to the total United States population (of all ages, races, residences, and classes). Differences are then crudely attributed to "cultural" factors.

We assert that no analysis of the Jews can be complete without *systematic* and *controlled* comparisons to non-Jews. We have documented how the analysis of Jews can be distorted without such comparisons. These will be illustrated below.

In the examination of Jewish communal life, we analyze the changing "cohesiveness" of the group. We investigate the intensity of cohesion in various spheres of activity. By cohesion we mean the extent and intensity of interaction *among* Jews and *between* Jews and non-Jews. Interaction occurs in families, in neighborhoods, where people work and go to school, in cultural and social activities. The greater the interaction in the largest number of spheres of activity, the greater the cohesiveness of the group.

In general, the findings of recent research have shown that the transformation of the American Jewish community involved some overall reduction of social, economic, political, and demographic differences between Jews and non-Jews. This reduction implies some convergences between Jews and others in family and marriage patterns, childbearing, socioeconomic characteristics, residential distribution, occupational and educational patterns. Parallels between the organizational and institutional structure of Jews and non-Jews have been noted.

Cultural similarities have been documented extensively. Nevertheless, a systematic and detailed examination of the evidence, comparing Jews to other white ethnics or to Protestants and Catholics, points to the unmistakable conclusion that American Jews remain different in every one of these critical features of communal life. The overall distinctiveness of Jews means more than absence of Jewish assimilation in America.

The distinctiveness of Jews has many and varied determinants. It is not simply a result of the lack of integration of a white immigrant group. Nor does discrimination against Jews or some definable set of Jewish values account for continued distinctiveness in America. While we do not yet have a clear or specific picture of why Jews are distinctive, we do know that the major factors are likely to be structural features associated with social class, family structure, and background characteristics rather than universal Jewish values or some psychological definable Jewish "mentality." Perhaps of greatest significance, the distinctive features of American Jewish life imply bonds and linkages among Jews which form the multiple bases of communal continuity. These ties and networks are deeply embedded in family life and in educational, occupational, and residential patterns. They do not appear to be transitional or marginal. They are reinforced by religious and ethnic communal behavior and cemented by shared life styles and values. Hence, Jews in America remain a distinct community despite the changes which have transformed them generationally and their Americanization.

The detailed analysis of the meaning of Jewish distinctiveness in America focuses on the contexts in which Jews interact with each other. These may be organized around three sets of issues:

(1)   Interaction (or Jewish cohesion) among Jews at the margins of the community;

(2)   the generational bases of group continuity (family and demographic issues);

(3)   the quality of Jewish life, focusing on issues of resources (education, occupation, and social class) and institutional as well as cultural bases (religion and ethnic ties).

These themes, as we will show, are interrelated but it is helpful

13

analytically to focus on each separately.

Jewish Cohesion and the Marginals

Our first theme is the examination of the contexts of interaction between Jews and non-Jews. In modern American society there have been increasing social contacts between Jews and others. The move away from the constraints of ascription to choices based on universalistic criteria has increasingly characterized Jews in the 20th century. This openness has meant choice in residence, marriage, jobs, and housing. These choices involve increasing social interaction with others and therefore higher rates of intermarriage, mobility, and residential integration, resulting in, so it is inferred, marginality to the Jewish community.

The mechanisms linking Jews to others are assumed to be college education and geographic mobility. In turn, patterns of interaction are presumed to be the consequence of the desire among Jews for assimilation and acceptance in the non-Jewish world. The move toward non-Jewish circles is expected to be all encompassing but is particularly conspicuous in choices of spouses, neighbors, and friends. Those who intermarry, who live in areas of low Jewish density, and young migrants are assumed to be less attached to the Jewish community and less Jewish in their behavior. By being on the margins, they are assumed to be in the forefront of assimilation. Hence, high rates of intermarriage, of residential integration, of migration are viewed as indicators of the weakening quality of Jewish life. For those who are at the center of Jewish interaction -- those who marry other Jews, live in Jewish neighborhoods, and remain in the local community, cohesion (i.e., interaction among Jews) is high. As the number and proportions of those on the margins increase, levels of Jewish cohesion are expected to decline on all other bases as well.

There is no question that there have been increases in intermarriage rates, in the migration of younger and older Jews, and in the residential integration of Jews and non-Jews in the neighborhoods of American metropolitan areas. There remain serious limitations to the specification of rates of change and levels attained. National patterns of intermarriage, residential integration, and migration remain unclear and variations among Jewish communities are difficult to interpret. Nevertheless, the critical questions have almost never been asked, since the answers

14

were obvious, assumed, or inferred. The two critical questions of relevance to policy concerns are:

(1)   What determines levels and changes in rates of intermarriage, residential integration, and migration?

(2)   What are the consequences of these patterns for the cohesion of the American Jewish community?

The first question has almost always been answered vaguely ("generational change", "assimilation") or in terms of values and attitudes (Jewish values on marriage and continuity are changing; Jews want to assimilate and desire integration). These responses are not helpful in clarifying the sources of change and continuity; in large part, they only rephrase the questions -- why do Jews want to assimilate? How and why does generational change lead to intermarriage? These questions have never been researched directly and have remained inferences from the changing patterns.

A systematic examination of the evidence on these issues suggests a significantly different picture of those on the margins. Some of the highlights of the data include the following.

(a)   There is no deep-rooted ideological base favoring out-marriage among Jews even among the out-married. There is no empirical confirmation that intermarriage simply reflects values and attitudes favoring assimilation. Gender and educational differences in intermarriage rates cannot be explained by differential values.

(b)   When the links between intermarriage and Jewish cohesion are measured directly (rather than *inferring* the levels of Jewish commitment from the rate of intermarriage) the evidence (not surprisingly) shows that the intermarried are less Jewishly connected. However, differences between the intermarried and the non-intermarried have *narrowed* over time as the rate of intermarriage has increased. In part, this is because the non-intermarried are secular and unaffiliated as well. Intermarriage, however, is not a causal factor in a general trend toward secularization and disaffiliation. It is not

15

particularly selective of the less committed. Ethnic and religious identification among young intermarried couples is not associated with disaffection from Judaism or the Jewish community through friends, neighbors, occupational networks, and Jewish cultural activities. Strong communal bonds and networks link the intermarried to the community.

(c)   The evidence shows that marriage between Jews and non-Jews is not necessarily the final step toward assimilation. Intermarriage does not inevitably imply the weakening of all communal attachments for the intermarried. In large part, data support the conclusion that the Jewish partner in an intermarriage remains attached to the Jewish community. In many cases, the non-Jewish born partner in an intermarriage becomes attached to the Jewish community through family, neighborhood, friends, organizations, religious and ethnic ties -- as do the children of the intermarried. Therefore, intermarriage in the United States in the 1970s and in the 1980s is likely to be a quantitative and qualitative gain for the American Jewish community. The quantitative losses assumed to result from intermarriage reflect a series of inferences derived from ideological and theological presuppositions which find little or no empirical support.

(d)   There is evidence as well ·that an increasing proportion of American Jews are accepting the intermarried within the community. While a preference for marriage between Jews continues to be expressed, there has been a major turn-around in the extent of rejection of the intermarried. Nevertheless, some indications persist that there remain formal-institutional and informal attitudinal barriers to the integration of intermarried families within Jewish communities. Many more of the intermarried identify themselves as Jews and are part of Jewish networks of family, friends, and neighbors than are associated formally (through membership or identification) with the religious and

16

social institutions of the community. Barriers to the formal (and in turn the greater normative) acceptance of intermarried couples who want to be part of the Jewish community need to be reduced in order to more fully integrate important segments of the community.

(e) Similar findings emerge from the analysis of others on the margin. For example, where Jews live and the Jewish density of their neighborhoods are significant factors in Jewish interaction with other Jews, with Jewish institutions serving the needs of the Jewish population, and the reinforcement of Jewish networks, shared life styles, values and norms. It remains empirically true that the higher the residential concentration of Jews, the greater the cohesiveness of the community measured in terms of formal ties to religious and social institutions. However, this does not seem to hold in terms of informal ties--it is no longer the case that the greater the residential dispersal and integration, the weaker the informal ties to the Jewish community. Nor does the recent evidence support the argument that those who are more mobile geographically have severed their Jewish communal ties.

(f) While high levels of Jewish density enhance certain kinds of cohesion, some important forms of Jewish cohesion are evident among those in areas of low levels of ethnic density. Similarly, while migration tends to reduce local community roots, these effects appear to be short-run. After a short period of time, 3-4 years, rates of Jewish communal participation and informal dimensions of Jewishness among migrants and non-migrants tend to be similar. The evidence from Jewish communities, as well as from more general studies of migration, shows that there are few long-term effects of migration on ethnic cohesion. There is also some evidence showing how new forms of communal growth follow from patterns of in-migration and increases in Jewish population density. Hence, while Jews have higher rates of geographic mobility than others, these patterns do not uproot and alienate Jews from their Jewishness.

(g)   Often the general data on the residential dispersion of Jews are compared to an idealized "standard" of total ghettoization. Of course, no one has seriously estimated the social, economic, and political costs of Jewish segregation. Such comparisons have always focused on the benefits but not the costs of residential segregation and the costs but not the benefits of integration -- hardly a balanced view. A systematic examination of the residential patterns of Jews and non-Jews in the United States as a whole as well as within communities shows continuous voluntary residential concentration among Jews. The distribution of Jews within metropolitan areas is by no means random. Nor are areas of high Jewish density characteristic only of the older, foreign born, poorly educated, lower class Jewish population. Areas of Jewish residential concentration in the last decade or so show increasing mixtures of age, generation, education, and social class. Jewish residential concentration is not a transitory phenomenon which is eroding continuously.

(h)   The determinants of intermarriage (as the determinants of marriage generally) are located in the contexts of where people meet (schools, jobs, neighborhoods), their socioeconomic backgrounds, and their cultural orientations. Desires for assimilation or Jewish values per se play a minor role for most American Jews. Similarly, factors associated with the residential patterns of Jews are not specifically Jewish. The "legacy" of the old world, the desire to live in Jewish areas, or the desire to escape from Jewishness, as well as specific values associated with Jewish residential concentration have all been invoked in past research as explanations for the distribution of Jewish population. Empirical tests of each one of these arguments fail to support any of these relationships. The factors clearly associated with the residential patterns of Jews are more general ones which characterize non-Jews as well -- housing markets, family life cycle, and economic constraints. Movement to areas of low Jewish density, as with

18

marriage choices, is not linked to a desire to assimilate or a search for social and residential contacts with non-Jews. Direct data on preferences, norms, and values show otherwise.

(i)   Unlike the patterns at earlier points in time and for different generations in America, the data show that community, defined geographically, is no longer the sole or major source of Jewish cohesion. Social ties and networks can be neighborhood based but are not necessarily. In the late 20th century, transportation and communication alternatives are substitutes for neighborhood based community. Jobs, life styles, and other social and cultural arenas are more important as bonds and linkages among Jews than residential clustering per se. Again, the definition of the Jewishness of the family in terms of biology (or Halacha) is becoming less important for most American Jews than it was in the past and less relevant to Jewish communal continuity than how people define themselves behaviorally, communally, and culturally, and how the community defines them.

Taken together, the variety of evidence about those who are on the margins of the Jewish community -- the intermarried, the migrants, and those in areas of low Jewish density -- does not reveal desires for assimilation or actual disengagement from the Jewish community. Policies need to target the marginal sectors of the Jewish population in ways which lead to their greater integration. General policies designed for the core of the Jewish community are not likely to reach the marginals.

Viewed in the context of the evidence and interpreted in the framework of Jewish cohesion, intermarriage needs to be understood less as a threat to Jewish continuity and more as a challenge for Jewish communal policies. As moving out of the parental home, like going to college, to the suburbs, or in the past moving to a new society, the normal structural supports for the intermarried are weaker. The challenge is to develop policies to build Jewishness on this new territory, as the Jewish community has done on other new territories. The objective is to create new institutions and networks that reinforce Jewishness on this new frontier. This challenge becomes an opportunity since intermarriage can be a source of demographic growth for American Jewry and, in turn, world Jewry.

Another conclusion derived especially from defining cohesion as interaction, is that policies aimed at the marginals should concentrate on magnifying interaction among Jews. This may result in the vacuity of Jewish organizational activities with little or no Jewish content. While Jewish organizations may want to offer a variety of significant Jewish educational and cultural opportunities (and should be encouraged to provide a wide range of Jewish educational and cultural experiences), the goal of providing contexts of interaction, sense of community, and alternative anchors of identity for Jewish marginals may be no less important. It is misdirected to evaluate policies directed at enhancing interaction among Jews at the margins by using ideal criteria of enriching Jewish cultural and ethnic-religious life. The appropriate standard for comparison is ignoring the marginals by developing no policies targeted for them. By that standard, enhancing interaction among Jews on the margins appears much more valuable. Moreover, providing a range of activities, from elementary forms of interaction to more intensive Jewish cultural and educational functions, combines wider communal coverage with in-depth options. What emerges, therefore, from social science research is the need to emphasize community among *all* the various segments. In that context, all the elements of communal life need to be included, from the elementary and trivial to the complex and profound.

Family and Generational Continuity

The family, marriage, childbearing, and household formation and dissolution are key themes in group life. Demographic continuity is the elementary form of group survival; links between the generations have been a major anchor of Jewish continuity. Is the Jewish family deteriorating? Are Jewish fertility rates below population replacement levels? Should the Jewish community be alarmed or concerned about the demographic survival of American Jews? Are family processes among Jews different than among non-Jews? Policies developed to "strengthen" the Jewish family or serve its needs must be based on an understanding of these issues. Investments to increase the Jewish birth rate or encourage larger Jewish families must be made after considering the evidence and evaluating the costs and probabilities of successful implementation.

20

The evidence to answer these questions shows that the family remains a powerful basis of community among Jews and continues to be one of the major sources of group continuity. Let us highlight some of the specifics:

(a) Jewish men and women continue to have lower divorce rates compared to other ethnics, despite increasing levels. Low divorce is a pervasive group characteristic, distinctive at all educational and social class levels. Thus, for example, higher education does not imply increased marital instability, and is therefore not a threat to Jewish family cohesion.

(b) In a similar way, no evidence is available to suggest high rates of permanent non-marriage among Jews. The extent of marriage is quite similar for Jews and non-Jews, as is the timing of marriage. Higher education among Jewish women, but not among Jewish men, results in delayed marriage, not non-marriage. Both the extent and the stability of marriage confirm the family-oriented characteristic of Jews. Marriage patterns imply generational ties and family connections. Linkages between families of different generations represent one continuing basis of cohesion among Jews, binding Jews together into a community. Educational attainment, unlike in the past, is not a threat to family-based Jewish cohesion.

(c) Family cohesion does not mean living in extended families. Most younger and older Jews, who are not married, live alone and not in families. In the trade-offs between family centrality and autonomy, the latter -- residential independence -- almost always is more powerful for Jews. However, the critical point about residential independence is that living away from family does not result in the deterioration of attachments to Judaism or Jewishness. There is no empirical relationship between living in non-family settings and Jewish cohesion. The data show that residential independence and Jewish continuity are not incompatible. This finding parallels the evidence discussed earlier on "marginal" Jews. The decline in

21

some aspects of family centrality as measured by living arrangements -- just as increases in intermarriage, migration, and residential integration -- has resulted in the development of new forms of group cohesion, particularly in friendship, neighborhood, religious, and ethnic ties, and not in alienation from the community.

(d)   The importance of the family does not mean large size. Jews have been characterized by lower fertility than non-Jews for over a century in the United States. Jewish women have about two children, on average, by the end of their childbearing period. Expected family size among younger married Jews (whose actual family size is incomplete) hovers around the two-child family. Similar levels of fertility expectations have been found among young unmarried adults. Assuming that these expectations are attained behaviorally, population replacement will occur. There is no evidence to support the fears of significant Jewish population decline in the next generation.

(e)   The concern has been often expressed that with higher educational levels and career commitments among young married Jewish women, fertility levels will decline below replacement levels. That pattern characterizes Protestant and Catholic women, but does not characterize Jews. The most educated Jewish women expect a larger family size than less educated Jewish women. Post-graduate education does not contradict eventual childbearing, even though it tends to alter the timing of marriage and the tempo of childbearing. Similarly, unlike non-Jewish women, there is no empirical relationship between the labor force participation of Jewish women and fertility expectations. Neither the educational attainment nor the career orientation of younger American Jewish women poses a threat to the demographic continuity of the American Jewish population.

There are many qualifications to the demographic data available which preclude systematic and detailed population projections as a basis for short-term population policy. Only very poor quality data are available on intermarriage and the eventual Jewishness of the children of intermarried couples; there are many unknowns about the eventual marriage patterns of currently non-married young persons; there are limitations to the use of expected family size data as predictors of actual fertility behavior. Nevertheless, when we evaluate the systematic and consistent evidence available on the demography of intermarriage and fertility, it becomes clear that predictions about the drastic numerical decline of the American Jewish population in the next generation is demographic nonsense. The small numerical declines predicted by the beginning of the 21st century may be balanced by Jewish immigration patterns, as it has in the last decade or so. Policy concerns about the demographic survival of American Jews are misdirected. There are several major demographic processes which should receive more policy attention. These are discussed below. Population growth and fertility levels are not, however, high on that list.

Quality of Jewish Life

There are two dimensions to the quality of Jewish life: (1) resources associated with the stratification and social class composition of the American Jewish population and (2) religious and ethnic communal bonds. The data available on major aspects of these two dimensions are relatively known, although often have been interpreted only within the narrow confines of the assimilation framework. We review briefly the evidence and suggest some new ways to interpret the emerging patterns. These interpretations have consequences for policy planning and implementation.

Changes in the stratification and social class networks have almost always been viewed in the context of the integration of ethnic immigrant groups. The upward mobility of Jews, their high educational attainment and occupational achievement have been viewed as indicators that Jews have "made it" in America. We emphasize related aspects of the occupational and educational transformation of the Jews: the concentration of Jews in particular occupations, linked to specific jobs, and the concentration of Jews among the college-educated, with college attendance among young Jews treated as a "given," not an option.

23

Indeed, the concentration of Jews among those with high levels of white collar occupations and college educations is a unique feature of the American Jewish community. Over 90 percent, and probably 95 percent, of young Jewish boys and girls graduate from high school and go on to college. Similarly, Jews are disproportionately concentrated in professional and managerial occupations and among those who have post-graduate levels of education. These socioeconomic levels characterize the Jewish population in America in ways which differentiate Jews from non-Jews. Indeed, the occupational and educational disparities between Jews and non-Jews have increased over time. In many ways, the educational attainment of American Jews increasingly differentiate them from other diaspora Jewish communities, and from Israeli Jews as well. Policies designed to encourage international networks among Jews need to take these patterns into account.

Emerging from the detailed evidence on particular occupations and patterns of self-employment is a portrait of the centrality of Jewish occupational linkages for institutions, networks, families, neighborhoods, life styles and political interests. These patterns of occupational concentration have become a powerful source of ethnic ties and interests. To interpret patterns of occupational mobility as "occupational assimilation" is to miss the important role of occupational concentration (even at higher social class levels) as a context of interaction and community. Ethnic cohesion among contemporary American Jews finds its primary source in the structural conditions of job and social class (and all the ramifications for interests, values, and life style) and not primarily in the search for ethnic identity or in the desire for group survival. To the extent that these occupational patterns are linked to life style and are fundamental arenas of group life (as are family patterns), they are not mainly social-psychological constructs or individual level motivations for survival. Jewish continuity in America is therefore not primarily contingent on the desires and motivations of Jews. The mobilization of these occupational networks and educational resources, within local American communities and among them, as well as between American Jewry and other Jewries, should be a major policy objective.

One of the immediate determinants of occupational concentration is educational attainment. At the same time that the educational gap between Jews and non-Jews has widened, the generational gap in educational attainment among Jews has

24

narrowed. The closer similarity between the generations in educational attainment implies important bonds which are family related. There is much less generational conflict currently among Jews as two generations -- men and women -- are college-educated. If in the past, particularly between the immigrant and second generations, educational accomplishments implied generational conflict (not necessarily over the value of education but over life style and interests), the educational homogeneity of the third and fourth generations implies the absence of this form of family tension and conflict. Hence, unlike the past, the educational attainment of Jews does not threaten the cohesiveness of the community. To the contrary: college educational experiences serve as powerful bonds between the generations. Again, American Jews are distinctive in these patterns, relative to non-Jewish white ethnics and relative to other Jewish communities (including Israel) around the world.

The concentration of Jews in occupational and educational categories goes well beyond crude classification. A detailed examination of specific professional activities and managerial positions reveals very high levels of concentration in particular fields and very low levels in other fields. There is as well a concentration of Jewish students in particular educational institutions related to concerns of quality and location. In turn, these patterns have consequences for Jewish density at colleges and hence for Jewish interaction and Jewish institutional presence on campuses.

Occupational and educational similarities among Jews of the same generation and between Jews of different generations imply networks, ties, and linkages among Jews; they imply commonalities of life styles and interests intragenerationally and intergenerationally. As such, they have become major sources of cohesion among American Jews.

The increasing educational and occupational disparities between Jews and non-Jews are vividly illustrated when we examine direct occupational and educational changes of two generations. For example, among Jews in the mid-1970s two-thirds of Jewish workers had sons who were professionals; two-thirds of the non-Jewish workers had sons who were workers. Similarly, the proportion of fathers with a high school education whose sons *only* had a high school education was 5 percent among Jews, 36 percent among Protestants and 55 percent among

25

Catholics. These generational patterns clearly reflect the crystallization of socioeconomic distinctiveness of Jews. These social mobility patterns have not led to the assimilation of Jews but to their differentiation from non-Jews.

Similar findings characterize the labor force and occupational patterns of Jewish women. Working outside the home has often been viewed as increasing the contacts between Jewish and non-Jewish women. But, as for men, occupational patterns of Jewish women tend to reinforce their contacts within their own ethnic group. An examination of work and educational patterns of Jewish women supports this argument. Self-employment and occupational concentration link Jewish women to each other, outside the family and neighborhoods. Hence, the work patterns of Jewish women reinforce ethnic networks rather than threaten ethnic cohesion.

The high levels of educational attainment and occupational achievements of American Jewish women pose particular challenges to policy. Past orientations of the organized Jewish communities in America to sex segregated activities (Temple sisterhoods; young women's affiliates of Jewish Federations) need to be reconsidered. Mid-week luncheon activities and afternoon teas exclude major sectors of Jewish women. While the issue of the career orientations of young Jewish women has often been discussed in the context of its consequences for the family -- the effects on delayed marriage, non-marriage, and childbearing -- the importance of the new labor force patterns of Jewish women is much broader. Two contexts are directly relevant: (1) the institutional context of Jewish organizations; (2) the links between Jewish women in the United States and Israel. Policies directed to the former issue are more likely to be successful, however difficult. The educational and occupational gaps between American women and their Israeli counterparts have widened in recent years and will increase even more in the next decades.

A second dimension of the quality of Jewish life relates to religious and ethnic factors. Often these are viewed as the cultural content of Judaism and Jewishness and as the social-psychological anchors of identity and identification. Religious and ethnic forms of behavior also represent structural contexts of interaction. The synagogue is not only a place to connect up spiritually and historically with Judaism or to perform particular rituals. It is also a place where social and economic contacts among Jews are made; it is a primary organizational context for Jewish interaction.

The evidence available confirms unambiguously declining religiosity and ritual practice among the younger generations. There seems to be little doubt about the growing secularization of American Jews. The data also document the emergence of a variety of new ethnic linkages, defining Jewishness beyond religion. The decline in one aspect of Judaism does not necessarily imply the decline in all aspects of Jewishness. Indeed, viewing the total array of social and cultural forms of Judaism and Jewishness, formally and informally, reveals the multiple bases of Jewish cohesion. These include in addition to religious dimensions (denominational affiliation and synagogue membership, ritual and holiday observances, and attendance at religious services) ethnic ties to Israel, Jewish friends and Jewish neighbors.

Despite the general decline in some traditional ritual observances, Jews have high levels of religious denominational identification. About three-fourths of adult American Jews identify themselves as Orthodox, Conservative, or Reform. Moreover, when focusing on those who do not identify themselves religiously, the non-affiliated, those on the margins religiously, most studies have been inferential: Non-denominationalism and non-affiliation equals assimilation. An empirical examination of the evidence suggests otherwise. The non-affiliated have Jewish friends and neighbors, are linked to each other, are involved with Israel and Jewish culture. There is no basis for concluding that religious decline means the absence of ethnic continuity.

When we take into account the wide range of social and cultural forms of Jewish expression--religious and ethnic--and include informal and formal networks and bonds, as well as family, occupational, and residential linkages, the multiple forms of cohesion characterizing American Jews and the deep-rooted anchors of Jewish continuity emerge clearly.

The detailed and consistent portrait of the American Jewish community drawn from a systematic examination of the evidence, and the interpretations which we have offered, do not imply that there is no basis for concern or no central role to policy and planning. There is no basis for complacency; there is no justification for self-congratulation. Nevertheless, the question has always been, what areas should be the focus of policy concerns?

The investment and policy planning in areas where there is less need or lower probability of successful implementation distracts from alternative investments in areas pinpointed by research to be of greater priority. The evidence points to new emerging patterns in the American Jewish community which require policy consideration.

The general evidence we have analyzed show that the linkages and networks among Jews are broader and deeper than has often been suggested. These formal and informal networks mean that the Jewish community is strong and vibrant. Jews are literate, intelligent, educated in secular and in Jewish studies. About three-fourths (perhaps more) of Jewish youngsters in America have exposure to Jewish education of some kind during their early years. Often we conceptualize Jewish education as a basis for Jewish continuity in narrow terms of quality and relative to the mythical images of the past. We ask, how many hours are spent, learning what materials, how good are the teachers and the program, how many years are Jewish youngsters exposed to the rich history and literature of the Jewish people? All these are reasonable (and often frustrating) bases for evaluation. But we often miss an important dimension of Jewish education (as we have of Jewish religious institutions): The contacts which occur among Jews in institutions of Jewish education. Clearly, interaction among Jewish youngsters occurs in Jewish educational institutions; but there is a much broader base of Jewish interaction there. Parents bring their children to school, have contact with other Jewish parents and with Jewish teachers and other Jewish children. The ramifications are extensive. It is clearly what community is all about. It may be that the specifics learned in a few hours of instruction are not very impressive, but it is also true that the Jewish educational context is a primary arena for Jewish cohesiveness. Once viewed in this perspective, the issues of American Jewish continuity become more than the casual dismissal of limited Jewish education or bemoaning the inadequacies of Jewish educational institutions, their staff, and their facilities.

Similarly, research studies have repeatedly documented the very wide observance of selected rituals, particularly Passover Seder and Hanukah candle lighting, and widespread attendance at religious services several times a year. These observances have often been dismissed as representing the secularization of religion and ritual -- the seder is "only" a family get-together for a meal

28

without its ritual richness or even its Kashrut observance; Hanukah was never celebrated to such an extent historically and reflects an acculturated response to Christmas; attendance at religious services occurs "only" a few times a year, the religious spiritual content has been deemphasized, and the social context is dominant. Nevertheless, it is an amazing fact of the 1980s that over three-fourths of American Jews are linked to each other in these ways. While the content of religious rituals and religious services has been transformed, these activities continue to bond Jews to each other, to their families and their communities, as well as to their culture, in profound ways. Whether these are linkages through family-centered activities, or through pride in Jewish victory, or through alternatives to non-Jewish rituals, they all serve as additional bases for communal cohesion. When, in addition, those who are not involved in these "religious" activities are involved in a variety of other "ethnic" and social activities which bring them into contact with other Jews, then the total community picture appears robust.

A similar argument can be made about the large proportion of American Jews who contribute time and money to Israeli-Jewish related causes and who visit Israel. These cannot be dismissed as "marginal." To the contrary. Israel is another anchor, a social and cultural connection, and an important basis for American Jewish communal life. Israel represents a basis of broad communal consensus among a wide range of Jews within the community. For some, it is another spiritual or educational anchor; for others, it provides cultural support, substituting for religious depth; still others find political and social significance in their identification with Israel and a major link to Jewish history and roots. Whatever Israel represents for individuals in America, it is perhaps the major locus of communal cultural or ideological consensus. As a result, the institutional and organizational structure of the community has focused on Israel (along with anti-semitism) to generate maximum communal integration. In turn, the formal institutional network has enhanced the conspicuousness and centrality of Israel in American Jewish life.

It is not clear whether the relationship of American Jews to Israel is more central for older than for younger Jews in the United States. Generational change and life cycle effects cannot be disentangled--i.e., it is unclear whether age differences should be interpreted as "change" or are associated with being "younger" or "older". It is therefore not clear whether the younger

29

generation will relate to Israel as they get older in ways that are similar to how the older generation currently relates to Israel. My assessment is that age differences are more likely to reflect life cycle factors and the relationship of the younger generation to Israel will increase as they move through the life cycle and as Israel and America change.

It is, of course, an error to assume that American Jews are bound to each other mainly by external sources (e.g., Israel) or the reactions of non-Jews to them (i.e., anti-semitism). They are bound to each other, more so now than in the past, by common life styles and networks, by positive sharing. Israel-American relationships need, of course, to reflect this *symmetry* rather than reflect the view that the American Jewish community is feeble and dying and that Israel is the only or major anchor for the American Jewish future. It is time that policies reflect the fact that the American Jewish community is a powerful source of vitality in world Jewry.

The longer range question is whether social networks and the constellation of family, ethnic, religious, and social ties will persist as bases of cohesion. How much secularization and erosion of traditional religious observances can occur without having an impact on generational continuity? Do new forms of Jewishness balance the secularization of Judaism? Will some "return to Judaism" or creative Jewish expression become a new core of generational continuity? As a community, Jews are surviving in America, even as some individuals enter and others leave the community. Policies need to be designed which reinforce the ethnic component of American Jewish continuity through an awareness of the positive features of modern Jewish communal life and through linkages to other Jewish communities in Israel and elsewhere. This is particularly the case for the various segments of the Jewish community which are defined as marginal or on the periphery.

Over the last decade, the changes characterizing the generations have resulted in greater ties among age peers and between younger and older generations. These generational continuities are clearly observed in occupational and educational concentration and dimensions of religiosity and ritual observances. The clashes and conflicts which characterized relationships between previous generations are no longer conspicuous features of generational relationships among contemporary American Jews.

Current social class and religious continuities between the generations imply greater family and social connections.

The oversimplified assimilation framework predicting the gradual and continuous erosion of Jewish cohesion is inconsistent with the empirical evidence. It is more accurate to understand the American Jewish community within a pluralistic framework which includes a focus on family ties, economic networks, social class bonds, educational background, and residential patterns linked to life style, interaction, and ethnic community.

Contemporary American Jews are clearly different from those of the past; so are their communities. To describe them in terms of assimilation is to miss the complexity of community and to obscure the major sources of cohesion. The social, economic, and political distinctiveness of Jews is characteristic of the contemporary American community no less than in the past, even though the forms of distinctiveness are different. Differences between Jews and non-Jews are neither trivial nor transitory; Jewish distinctiveness serves as a major basis for group continuity. To assume that policies need to be designed as emergency brakes against the inevitable assimilation of American Jews is misdirected. To ignore the major strengths of the American Jewish community in the design of policy is to fail to build on and enhance the quality of Jewish life.

III. POLICY PERSPECTIVES

Policy Orientations, Targets, and Goals

How do the results of recent social scientific evidence on American Jews orient us to policy issues? We start by listing out below several key points of policy orientation. By policy orientation, we mean guidelines and choices which have to be made in designing policies for the community. In particular, we focus on the targets and goals of policy, so that there is a continuous feedback process from research to policy. Since the American Jewish community is continually undergoing change, policies need to be designed and redesigned to take into account these continuous change processes. Without some notion of targets or objectives, policy can never be evaluated.

What are the objectives of policy for the American Jewish community? They are difficult to specify unambiguously. They are likely to differ among Jewish leaders and institutions in America and in Israel. Certainly the emphasis and priorities will vary. Goals are also shaped by the constraints -- social, economic, ideological, and political -- in the implementation of policies. Nevertheless, as a basis for evaluation and discussion, policy objectives need to be articulated.

Three broad goals may be identified which seem to encompass most of the specific policy implications derived from research.

(1)   Policies should be designed to enhance the cohesion of the Jewish community. By this we mean that the many and diverse ways which reinforce the interaction of Jews with other Jews should be a fundamental goal of Jewish policies.

33

These include formal and informal structures of interaction.

(2)   As a community, policies should be directed to the enhancement of generational continuity. There are two major parts to continuity: demographic and cultural. Families (their formation and importance) are major aspects of demographic continuity; Jewish education in its broadest meaning is a critical mechanism of cultural continuity. Hence, policies should be directed to enhancing family and Jewish educational continuities.

(3)   Enhancing the multiple and varied forms of relationships to Israel is a third major objective of policy. These relationships cannot be limited to immigration (Aliya) policies or to asymmetrical patterns wherein American Jews contribute economically in exchange for "Jewish identity" and Israeli culture. They should include partnership and reciprocity which emphasize joint ventures and personal contacts.

These three goals are sufficiently broad and abstract to allow for maximum flexibility as well as for fundamental consensus. Policies which encompass more than one of these goals are most desirable. Again, it is important to stress that these goals are not necessarily substitutes for other goals.

Who are the target populations for policies? This question does not address the "who is a Jew" issue. We define a Jew in the broadest sociological sense of someone who defines him/herself as Jewish and is defined by others as Jewish. Rather we need to identify the various sectors within the Jewish community and target policies accordingly.

A series of complex choices are involved in the selection of the target population(s) for policy. Each of the potential choices has advantages and disadvantages and there is little evidence from research to help clarify the priorities among them. For example, it is relatively clear from the evidence that community level interaction and networks are fundamental sources of Jewish identification. Moreover, variation among communities is substantial. Policies directed at enhancing interaction at local levels are more likely to be implemented than at the national level. Often patterns examined at the national level neutralize the variation among communities and minimize existing heterogeneity. Policies, therefore, can be most effective and implemented at the local communal level. These and related concerns point to targeting the local community for policy development. However, focusing only on the local community misses important patterns of linkages among communities (e.g., internal migration and intercommunity economic and family networks). There are also important patterns (e.g., relationships to Israel) which transcend local community variation. And, of course, there are many economic and political reasons to coordinate policy development among communities.

The choice of targeting policies nationally or locally, taking into account advantages and disadvantages, is not simple. Nevertheless, policies developed which are not sensitive to the heterogeneity among communities and which do not take into consideration the problems of implementation for a community which is organized loosely on a voluntary basis are not likely to have a major impact. A neglected element in the choice between national and local targets is the need to focus policy on the *linkages* among communities. Family, economic, and educational patterns among Jews have already connected them across local community boundaries. Migration patterns associated with economic opportunities, occupations and careers, as well as of the young for educational purposes and of the older population in search of leisure and retirement (either as temporary, seasonal movers or as permanent settlers in the warmer sunbelt) imply new types of relationships beyond the local community. Focusing on the local community often narrows our view; focusing only on the national community blurs our vision of the particular and of heterogeneity. As a balance, policies should also be directed to the ties and bonds across communities.

Another set of choices about targeting policies relates to whether they are designed to address the core Jewish population (i.e., those who are at the center of Jewish communal activity, whose bases of cohesion are intensive and extensive) or those who are at the margins. It is clear that these sectors need first to be identified. Policies addressed to one sector may not be appropriate for the other; methods of implementing policies for those in the core are not likely to be as effective for those on the margins and vice versa. A similar set of choices relates to targeting social-demographic sectors of the Jewish population, particularly those associated with the life cycle. Policies for the young and older ages, for the married with and without children, need to be

35

specified. Changes over the life cycle are critical orientations for policy, planning, and implementation.

There are comparable policy choices regarding the formal and informal sectors of the community. Obviously formulating and implementing policies for those who are affiliated and involved in the institutional structure are easier tasks than designing policies for the non-affiliated. Moreover, focusing solely on the organizational context of community life misses the centrality of informal networks -- economic, residential, occupational, and social -- which define the Jewish community.

Arenas for Policy Development

What particular dimensions of social life should be the concern of policies? Having defined some broad objectives of policy and identified the population(s) targeted for policy concerns, we need to consider briefly the various social, economic, political, and cultural dimensions of Jewish communal life where policies should focus. These dimensions will be referred to as arenas for policy development.

The first arena for policy development relates to the *Jewish family*. While in the past, policy pronouncements have been directed toward "strengthening" the Jewish family, the evidence available suggests that American Jews are very family oriented, that family ties are strong, within and between generations. There are several policy issues, however, which require a focus on the family. These are highlighted below since they have been discussed substantively earlier.

Policy needs to focus on the family life cycle, in particular on those parts of the age transitions where Jews live outside of families. These time periods of living alone are increasing among American Jews as among others. In particular, younger persons often leave home between the end of high school and before beginning a family of their own. This pattern is relatively new; in the past, most remained in the parental home until they married. Residential independence among American Jewish young adults has increased. Similarly, divorced, previously married persons, and the non-married tend to live in non-family settings. Older persons, who are no longer married, are more likely to live alone than either in institutions or as part of an extended family. Given differential mortality patterns of men and women, a significantly

36

higher proportion of older persons are widowed women. Most of these live alone.

Services and broader policies need to be designed for these new family life cycle transitions. Targeting age groups before marriage or the never married and previously married is a major challenge to policies which in the past have focused on the family as the major target or treated the non-married as temporary and deviant. Non-family residential patterns have become important for various segments of the life cycle and need to be considered in policy formations.

A second family-related arena for policy focuses specifically on the changing role of Jewish women. Changes in the timing and tempo of childbearing among American Jewish women and their growing commitments to careers outside of the family, require new policy orientations. Traditional organizational activities have to be reoriented. Sex-segregated activities have to be reconsidered. Work related networks among Jewish women need to be established and reinforced as they have among Jewish men in the past. The different labor force patterns of Jewish women compared to others (the later peaks of participation, fluctuations in conjunction with childbearing, and re-entry) need to be identified and considered in planning activities. Successful organizational models which have worked very well in the past are unlikely to work well in the future. Even when they meet the needs of some sectors of the population, large and growing sectors of women are excluded.

A third part of the family arena relates to intermarriage. Rates of intermarriage are likely to remain high, with a great deal of fluctuation by area and community. While there is reason to be wary of most (if not all) of the intermarriage data currently available, enough is known to suggest that the quantitative and qualitative issues are not as alarming as has often been portrayed. Indeed, there is some evidence indicating important contributions of the intermarried, demographically, socially, and culturally, to American Jewish life. Nevertheless, there is every reason to focus on the consequences of intermarriage and to follow up on the children of intermarried couples. While there is growing acceptance of the intermarried within the Jewish community, formal institutional affiliation remains weak. There is also some data which indicate a feeling of communal rejection felt by the intermarried. Major policy attention should be directed to uncover ways to better integrate the marginal intermarried in formal and informal ways. They are a major resource, insufficiently appreciated, by the leadership of the American Jewish community (and by the Israeli Jewish population as well).

A second major arena of Jewish policy is *Jewish education.* While there are many who have focused on this policy area, we direct attention to the interactional value of the Jewish educational experience. In particular, there is need to focus Jewish educational activities (in the broadest sense) on teenagers and college students. These age segments represent potential detachments from the family and the organized Jewish community. Traditional institutional responses to these groups have met with but moderate success (if at all). College and post-college young adults are the least likely to be responsive to traditional educational approaches. Jewish institutions are not structured to address these issues. They do not compete well with the challenges of general educational institutions. The incorporation of the Jewish with general institutions is one possibility. In particular, the focus of Jewish education on the positive side of Jewish life and on contemporary Jewish communities needs to be developed. These should be targeted to college age populations.

Programs to link American Jewish college students to the variety of academic and non-academic programs in Israel have proliferated in recent years. New programs not focused directly on post-high-school-pre-college or on a junior year abroad or on the more committed, core of American Jewish youth need to be developed.

A third arena of policy development should deal with the *demography* of Jewish Americans, taking into account the broadest range of population related issues and addressing real problems. In the past, quantitative or demographic issues were thought to revolve around issues of the size of the American Jewish population and particularly its low fertility level. Evidence shows unmistakably that these are neither problems nor amenable to policy manipulation. While Jewish fertility is low, it has been low for several decades. There is, in addition, little that can be done to increase the Jewish birth rate. Investments in this area are not likely to have measurable effects and are misdirected. This is particularly the case since those with lower fertility are the marginals who are least likely to be affected by general policies.

38

Important demographic issues revolve around migration, the emergence of new Jewish communities, and the ties among Jewish communities. We know little about the effects of temporary-seasonal movements of older persons and are just beginning to understand the importance of the migration of the young in the transition to adulthood. While I cannot foresee any policy which will reverse these patterns (nor should they), policy should be concerned with the greater integration of the migrants within the community. Policy should focus on ways to reduce the marginality of the migrants at all ages. One example relates to college students. Jewish communities have generally viewed college students as transients in their community, non-contributors to their institutions, and have, as a result, ignored their presence. The local Jewish campus institution (e.g., Hillel) tends to focus on campus needs, in isolation from the community. Often the only linkage of Hillel to the Jewish community is as recipient of funds or as a mobilizer of Jewish students to collect money for Jewish charities or Israel. There are more creative ways to develop opportunities, formal and informal, within the Jewish community to enhance the interaction between college students and the local Jewish community. While the forms of such linkages will vary by community structure, size, and the nature of local colleges and universities, there is room for major institutional developments to enhance the greater integration of these "temporary migrants" into the Jewish community. A new liaison organization might be established which would be a clearinghouse of linkages between students and the local Jewish community. This would involve linking students to volunteer activities, service, or "needs" of the community, and link the community to the needs of students beyond the campus.

Another demographic theme of importance relates to the changing profile of some communities, particularly the pattern of aging. Much programming has been addressed to the various services provided for the elderly by the community. Less attention has focused on the sex composition of the older population (the very large proportion of women) and the patterns of residential independence among the non-married older Jewish population.

A major issue in American Jewish demography is the immigration of significant numbers of Russian Jews and Israelis in the recent decade. In addition to the integration of the Russians within the Jewish community, much more policy attention should be addressed to the American-Israeli population. They remain out of the mainstream of the American Jewish community. They are in the anomalous situation of being Hebrew-speaking Jews, closely linked to each other and with Israel, but clearly not integrated into the Jewish communities where they live. The potential they represent as bridges between American Jews and Israel has not been exploited. Indeed, the negative view of Israeli Jews toward those who immigrate to America has all too often affected the American Jewish view. These need to be reconsidered from *both* Israel's view and the American Jewish perspective. It should be part of a clear policy direction toward greater symmetry in Israeli-diaspora relationships. Just as American Jewish emigration to Israel is a powerful bond between the American Jewish community and Israel, the reverse (Israeli Jewish immigration to the United States) should be viewed as a cross-national bond fostering new networks of interaction.

An emphasis within demographic research is the importance of understanding cohort or generational patterns as well as the effects of periods of time. The generational shifts which have occurred in America (and elsewhere) constitute another important arena for policy development. A new generation is emerging in America which has particular social and economic characteristics and family experiences, radically different from previous generations. Not only have they not had direct contact with major events of contemporary Jewish history (for example, the establishment of Israel, the holocaust) but they have grown up in an environment of relative affluence, secularization, higher education, middle class occupations, women's liberation, and individualism (among others). Policies which do not take these new developments into account directly are less likely to have an impact. Policies which may have worked in the past will not necessarily be appropriate in the future, as the community has changed in composition and orientation.

A final arena of policy development focuses on the variety of resources characteristic of American Jews. In particular, policies need to take into account the power, education, and the Jewishness of American Jews. There is a need to mobilize occupational networks and educational resources in ways that go beyond the economic. There is much expertise among American Jews which has not been sufficiently tapped by the Jewish institutional structure. There has been a continuous strain between the formal institutional structure of the Jewish community and more educated Jewish Americans. While in previous generations, educational attainment, particularly graduate level, tended to be exceptional among Jews as among others, this is no longer so. This is true for Jewish women and men. New ways need to be found to develop mechanisms for the utilization of this powerful resource in enhancing the quality of Jewish life.

Three Policy Recommendations

In this section, we present three specific policy suggestions. These are based on the implications of our research and attempt to link the emerging social patterns among American Jews to specific policies. Each policy suggestion combines several major themes and targets specific subpopulations among Jews. The suggestions are:

(A) Summer program for unaffiliated young Jews;

(B) support for the development of modern Jewish studies nationwide on college campuses;

(C) the development of new relationships among the Jewish leadership in Israel and the United States.

We detail these proposals below, without regard to priorities among them. Obviously, it is my feeling that these policies are worthwhile, but they were not designed necessarily as substitutes for existing policies or for alternative policies that may be developed. They should be viewed as suggestive.

A. Summer Program for Unaffiliated Teenagers

One of the fundamental questions which emerges from social science research revolves around those on the margins. While it is relatively easy to define policies and implement planning procedures for those who are affiliated with the Jewish community, formally or informally, it is much more difficult to identify, let alone reach and have an impact on, those who by their characteristics and behavior are not part of the core community. Although research has demonstrated that those on the margins are not totally alienated from all community attachments, they are particularly difficult to involve in the

41

community per se. Since policy tends to be formal and planning tends to be institutional, those on the margins are least likely to be reached by general policies designed for the total population. The dilemma is how to set up a policy addressed specifically to those on the margins of the Jewish community.

The following outline suggests one way to target the non-affiliated, involve them in Jewish activities, increase a sense of communal involvement for the community as a whole, enhance the relationship between the affiliated and the marginals, emphasize the communal aspects of Jewish education, and reinforce the bonds linking American Jews to contemporary Israeli society and to Jewish history. A bold policy is needed to meet these goals successfully.

We start by defining an activity which is of sufficient attraction, yet of educational and communal value. We propose that a one-month summer activity be designed to attract the teenaged (pre-college) children of the unaffiliated (aged 13-17). The activity should expose these teenagers to Jewish culture and history, providing a sense of togetherness and shared experience, i.e., a sense of community. It should involve a block of time where there is minimal competition from other academic work or social activities. It should take place where learning about Jewishness is less focused on a formal curriculum than on experiences. Hence, it is natural that such an activity should occur in Israel.

Let us deal with several specifics:

(1) The summer program should be designed for the unaffiliated. Hence, the first issue is how to reach them. One way is to advertise in local newspapers; another is to depend on informal networks. The program should address those who have had no or minimal attachments to the Jewish community; whose parents are unaffiliated, organizationally or religiously. The marginal can then be defined broadly in terms of the intermarried, those without communal memberships, the single-parent households, and so on.

(2) The attractiveness to the potential target population is that there would be *no fee* charged for a month of summer activity. It would be "free" from the point

42

of view of the participant. This should be an iron-clad rule; no exceptions. The program should be removed as far as possible from one dominant image of the organized community, as well as one association of American Jews with Israel -- fund-raising. Eligibility for participation is marginality to the Jewish community. It is a form of outreach program for the Jewishly disadvantaged.

(3)   The program itself should develop a broad-based agenda incorporating specific religious or Zionist orientations, but should not be confined to any one orientation. It should present, educate, discuss the rich array of history, culture and society associated with Jews and their communities. For the participants, the program should be a cafeteria of experiences. Israel is a mechanism for conveying a set of intense Jewish experiences but not an end in itself. It is a vehicle to foster awareness of Jewishness and a context of interaction for American Jewish youth who do not have other forms of Jewish interaction in America.

(4)   Each Jewish community should decide on its own how to define marginality (within general guidelines) and decide on the numbers and persons eligible. The organized Jewish community must be involved in order to represent the beginning of contact, and subsequent interaction, with the currently non-affiliated. The follow-up with the non-affiliated families and children would be a fundamental feature of integrating the marginals.

There is hardly a need to justify the focus on Israel as a setting for American Jewish youth or on the unaffiliated. Suffice it to note the enormous range of experiences, history and excitement that Israel can provide. The emphasis on learning about Jewishness and Judaism from being in Israel (rather than only about Israeli society or Zionism) complements the broader goal of fostering a sense of community attachment. Teaching through experience is more constructive (i.e., less threatening) than textbooks and classroom structure. It is a beginning rather than a complete process; it is to whet the appetite, display the range of culture and history rather than teach a particular

43

ideology or theological variant. It is primarily to foster Jewish interactions.

The orientation solely to the unaffiliated may raise questions about the special privileges and rewards for being marginal. Yet, I think there are advantages to targeting the marginals, since in this context it is of lower priority to provide alternative summer programming for the affiliated. I would be concerned that a general focus on Jewish teenagers rather than a specific focus on the marginals would be less successful from the point of view of a shared Jewish community experience for the marginals. Initial segregation may enhance subsequent integration. It may even generate competition for the affiliated to develop parallel programs.

It seems to me that the proposed program has a wide range of attractive qualities for many segments of the Jewish community. I list them briefly.

* It links American Jewish youth to Israel;

* it focuses on Jewish educational experiences;

* it maximizes the interaction among Jewish youth;

* it may serve as one bridge between the marginal adults (i.e., parent(s) of the participants) and the organized Jewish community in terms of a positive experience for their children;

* it mobilizes the organized Jewish community to identify and target policies for the most unreachable segments;

* it could provide employment for Jewish professionals (e.g., teachers) during a summer month -- linking them to Israel as well;

* it focuses on a life cycle stage of importance where Jewish educational experiences tend to be minimal.

There are two questions about the proposal, but they appear to me to be relatively minor: (1) Can such a program successfully reach the marginals? (2) Can costs be covered? To answer the first question, we should consider the following. There are less than a dozen American Jewish communities (even subdividing New York and Los Angeles) with more than 100,000 Jewish population. If we assume that each of these large Jewish centers contributes 75 Jewish teenagers to the program, that would cover about 800-900 participants. There are over 250 local Jewish communities in the United States with a range of population sizes. If 10-15 participants are selected from each, there can be an additional 2,500-3,000 teenagers. That is surely a grand beginning numerically -- perhaps it should be one-fifth the size. In any case, there are sufficient numbers of unaffiliated Jewish teenagers who can be located through advertisements, networks, informal contacts, etc.

Each community would be asked to cover the costs of their participants. In terms of the potential pay-offs in subsequent commitment, I cannot imagine that the returns would be lower than current investments in the Jewish education of pre-teenagers. My guess is that cost per participant would not exceed $2,000. for a month.[1]

While the specific policy outline focuses on teenagers, there are other persons who are part of the segment which we have defined as marginal. There are non-affiliated (and/or intermarried), post-college adults, single (non-married and previously married) adults, and older persons whose ties to the Jewish community have been marginal. Policies directed to them with some variant of that proposed for teenagers might represent the beginning of greater attachments for these segments. Given the centrality of increasing cohesion among those on the margins and linking Jews to each other (among communities in the United States and between America and Israel), this policy should be given highest priority.

It should be noted that we do not have detailed and systematic evidence showing the effects of participation in Israeli

----

[1] When evaluating the cost, the real question becomes what are the alternative uses for resources and what would it cost (in whatever terms can be measured) for not attempting policies which integrate the marginals.

45

programs (of all kinds) on subsequent Jewishness. As an integral part of this policy, I suggest that a research-evaluation section be built-in to learn if and how the experience has had an impact. Few Jewish policy programs have been evaluated and this is a reasonable demonstration project for systematic follow-up.

B. Modern Jewish Studies

Several major analytic themes provide the context and justification for the second policy suggestion.

The extent and quality of Jewish education in the United States have always been high among policy concerns. While there is a general consensus that there is room for improving the quality of the Jewish educational experience as well as the amount of hours spent, we have argued as well for the broadest treatment of the context of Jewish education. Jewish education provides a primary environment for interaction among Jews, including not only among students but among parents and between them and Jewish professionals. We now want to consider other institutional contexts (not only Jewish institutions) and other age groups (not only pre-teens) or "adult" education. In particular, we need to develop policies which relate to the age span 17-22 in non-traditional institutional contexts.

To these considerations we add a theme which relates to the sources of strength within the American Jewish community. While Israel and the holocaust provide some anchors for Jewish continuity in America, they are either external or negative (i.e., Jewish survival in America is dependent on the Jewishness of the Jewish state and the negative lessons of the holocaust). There are more powerful and positive themes about sources of cohesion in American society which need to be emphasized. Jewish educational experiences would be enhanced by a focus on the positive features characterizing the Jewish community in America.

In addition, we note the large number and very high proportion of Jewish teenagers in colleges. Many, but not all, are living away from home, even if temporarily. Leaving the supportive environment of home and community and moving to new areas requires special planning.

Formal Jewish institutional supports often are available on college campuses and serve important social, religious, and ethnic needs. There is also an academic gap that has rarely been recognized or filled. This gap is rarely of concern to local Jewish communities who tend to have marginal interest in transient college students whose families live elsewhere.

Based on the desirability of enhancing Jewish education in non-traditional contexts, designed for college students, with an emphasis on community in the broadest sense, we propose the following: the development, enrichment, support and growth of modern Jewish studies on American campuses. These programs can be organized within existing academic units. The association of Jewish studies with texts and the ancient world has a long academic tradition. We think there is a growing need to extend Jewish studies to incorporate systematically contemporary Jewish communities, in terms of traditional modern Jewish history courses plus courses on modern Jewish societies and politics. These could of course cover areas within social science and the humanities. The intellectual and academic justifications for such programs have been developed in other contexts. The policy emphasis here is in the value of such programs for the Jewish community. It could involve one link between the college student and research in the local community.

How can the Jewish community influence the curriculum and organization of studies in American universities? The answer is complex but involves endowments for professors, sponsorship of lectures, provision of research funds to study local communities. While these activities and courses would be open to all and need to be legitimate within the academic enterprise, they can be influenced by local communities and national policies. Israeli studies and holocaust courses could fit into such an emphasis. The presence of significant programs and courses on the campus, in a non-religious or social setting, legitimated by the academic community, in areas of study not limited to texts or the ancient world, might have an important impact on the awareness among Jewish students of their own culture and community. It may as well enhance the developments which are already occurring to link American college students to a broad range of programs in Israel.

C. Leadership Issues in Israel and America

The transformation of the American Jewish community has altered the ties and networks among Jews within the United States and between them and Jewries in Israel and elsewhere. It

47

is beyond the scope of this essay to consider the comparative transformations of Jewish communities around the world. Yet, it is of critical significance to involve issues associated with Israel in our focus on American Jews. This is the case because Israel is one anchor for the American Jewish communal consensus and an important part of the complex elements that are involved in the Jewishness of American Jews. Along these lines, we have specified that the strengthening of American-Israel connections (in the widest sense) is one of the major objectives of policy.

The issue of Israel-American relationships and policies associated with that relationship are part of the agenda of many Jewish institutions in America and Israel. Policies to enhance, intensify, clarify, justify, and expand the contexts of these cross-national relationships have been made. This is not the appropriate forum to summarize or evaluate these policies. We focus here on one small corner of policy in this area which relates to the changing patterns of leadership and their implications for Israel-American Jewish relationships.

In the past, there were major commonalities of background and experience between the leadership of the American Jewish community and Israel. Both were heavily influenced by, and directly sensitive to, their European (largely Eastern) origins; many were raised in families where Yiddish was spoken and were rooted in Yiddish culture; many struggled with second generation status, upward social mobility, and generation conflict. Many shared the cultural and social disruptions of secularization and assimilation. Most importantly, they shared the struggles of economic depression, war, and the holocaust in Europe, and the rebuilding of the lives of refugees. They shared in most tangible and dramatic ways the establishment and rebuilding of the State of Israel.

They also shared limited exposure to formal Jewish education; Jewish religious observances were rejected as part of the past, while national-Jewish rituals were developed as replacements. As American Jews became less traditionally oriented by becoming American, Israelis became less traditionally oriented by becoming attached nationally to their new country. The processes were similar and communication between them was based on a shared sense of origin and objective.

A new generation of Jewish leaders is emerging in America and Israel who are more distant from Europe, from ethnic language commonalities, from holocaust and immigration, from the struggles of pioneering and upward mobility. The differential experiences of the societies where Israeli and American Jews grew up, in their communities and the broader society of which they were a part, in the different roles of war and radical social changes in their lives and the lives of their children have the potential of driving wedges in their relationships.

Not only have the older commonalities of background and experience changed but new gaps have developed between American Jewish and Israeli leadership. Four major developments are among the most conspicuous:

(1)   American Jewish women have been in the forefront of social changes in the liberation from traditional sex roles and families. Their high levels of education and career orientations, their small family size and individual aspirations (for themselves and their children), have been thoroughly documented. In contrast, Israelis women tend to be much more traditionally oriented in terms of family and gender roles and in particular in terms of status as wife, daughter, worker, etc.

(2)   A second related shift involves the growing dominance of non-European origin Israelis born in Israel. This dominance is demographic as well as in terms of selected political and economic activities. The shift in Israel's ethnic composition creates at both the leadership and general population levels new gaps between them and American Jews. Differences are not only cultural but social and economic as well.

(3)   These growing gender and ethnic differences between the Israeli Jewish and American Jewish communities are tied in with the growing educational discrepancies between the two communities. While American Jews -- men and women -- are characterized by two generations of college exposure, such is the case for but a limited segment of the Israeli Jewish community. And that of course is further exacerbated when gender and ethnic origins are considered.

(4)   These complexities are related to the occupational concentration of American Jews (again men and women) in

49

professional and managerial positions, sharply distinct from the fuller occupational range among Israeli Jews.

In part these discrepancies and gaps reflect the minority position of Jews in America (relative to the dominance of Jews in Israel), the particular immigration history of Israel, and broader macro-societal features of the United States and Israel. Nevertheless, the growing commonalities among the generations of Jews in America in occupation, social class, education, culture and life style contrast sharply with the increasing American-Israel gap in these areas.

There is a more subtle gap which I think has not been adequately recognized. If we examine the characteristics of the leaders of Israeli and American Jews in various areas of social, political, cultural and economic activity, we might conclude that the characteristics of the elite in both societies were quite similar. That conclusion would be misleading since it ignores the macro context. While current characteristics of individuals might be similar, their backgrounds, experiences and societal context are different. For example, while both American Jewish and Israeli Jewish leadership of the new generation have relatively high levels of education, the American Jewish leadership is representative in education levels of the broader American Jewish population. The Israeli educated are an educated elite. Higher education is an exception among Israelis, while normative and typical among American Jews.

It is difficult to define sharply the "leaders" of the Jewish community in America (no less so in Israel). But it is likely that religious leaders -- of institutions, organizations, and synagogues -- would be among the defined leadership in America. The political and politicized nature of religion in Israel and the control exercised by one segment of the religious spectrum precludes serious communication among the religious leaders in both societies. While there is substantial evidence that the Jewish populations of Israel and America have similar patterns of religiosity, the leadership gap in the area of religion is substantial. This leadership gap is further widened when the important and increasing roles of Jewish women in economic, religious and social activities in America are considered. There seems to be nothing comparable to these changes within Israel.

These considerations underlie a third policy recommendation: to develop new ways to identify the next generation of leaders in both societies and implement programs to overcome some of the increasing gaps between them. While the leadership among American Jews has Israeli society high on the agenda, it is unlikely that Israeli leaders have American Jewry high on their agenda, outside of economic and political concerns. There are grounds for the development of greater symmetry in the relations between Israeli and American Jews.

There are few ways to develop policies to overcome the widening gaps in the leadership of the two communities. There is, however, an overwhelming need to educate both leadership groups about each other. American Jews tend to learn about Israeli society in the broadest sense (for personal, social, religious, and cultural reasons as well as economic and political); the relationship of Israeli Jews (and its leadership) to the American Jewish community tends to be more narrow. Policies need to be developed in ways which involve Israeli leadership in the wider range of Jewish, cultural, and social activities of American Jews. A greater appreciation of the rich Jewishness of American Jewish life, the cultural and social cohesion of the community, and the diversity of religiosity and ethnic expression of American Jews would go far in bridging a widening gap. It would move both communities toward greater symmetry and hence toward greater cohesion.

As with many policy recommendations, the long-term issue of these three policy proposals relates to the allocation of scarce resources. These general policy proposals and other suggestions made throughout this essay require careful and systematic allocation of funds, probably allocated from other alternative programs or service activities. Who is to say whether resources should be poured into universities to research the local community or send the children of the unaffiliated to Israel or focus on symmetrical relations among the leadership and elites of American Jewry and Israel? How do these recommendations compete with improving salaries for Jewish teachers, settling old-new immigrants in Israel, helping the Jewish poor and aged, counseling Jewish families, and carrying out scientific research in Israel? There are no simple ways to set policy priorities, to estimate and evaluate the relative success of policy, or to decide how best in the interest of the community to spend funds. Nor are guidelines available from research that help identify the relative importance of project A or B or the most cost-effective ways to produce results x, y, or z.

It is easier to raise policy issues than to address these difficult trade-offs. Throughout we have raised questions about the policy implications of changes in women's roles, the integration of the intermarried, the mobilization of occupational and educational networks, the use of the potential resources available among American Jews, the mushrooming of new American Jewish communities through migration, and the ways in which Israeli society and American Jewry form mutually reinforcing linkages. There are no clear policies to deal with these issues. I am convinced, however, that an informed and systematic picture of the American Jewish community is the necessary first step toward the articulation of policies and their evaluation. As new evidence is gathered, digested, and analyzed we shall need to reassess our policies and our priorities repeatedly. As we keep the links between research and policy strong, our policies can be better evaluated and goals more clearly attained.

PART TWO

RESPONSES AND COMMENTARIES

Reuven Hammer
Rita E. Hauser
Harold S. Himmelfarb
Richard G. Hirsch
Wolfe Kelman
Deborah Dash Moore
Bernard Reisman
Jonathan D. Sarna
Alexander Schindler
Charles E. Silberman
Ira Silverman
Jacob B. Ukeles

REUVEN HAMMER
The Jewish Theological Seminary of America
(Jerusalem Center)

Since I am not a social scientist or demographer, I cannot possibly dispute the figures and statistics of this paper, nor would I want to. I assume that they are correct and that the general conclusion of the paper to the effect that the American Jewish community is neither dying nor doomed, that the reports of its death have been greatly exaggerated, is factually correct. This is a conclusion which all of us should welcome. I have long suspected that the figures we have heard are exaggerated and that there is a misguided effort on the part of over-zealous propagandists to convince everyone that that is the case. Negative Zionism has been built upon two points: anti-semitism and assimilation. Since anti-semitism is now not a realistic problem in America, the emphasis has been put upon assimilation. The truth is that the problems of assimilation are real enough and difficult enough without exaggerating them needlessly and falsely. I do not believe that it is necessary to build Zion upon the death of another community.

The second point of the paper is the assertion that the American Jewish community is cohesive, powerful, flourishing and creative. I cannot help but feel that the statement that the American Jewish community is "entering a period of flourishing and creative development" is as much an exaggeration as the opposite view which the paper refutes. It may indeed be a consummation devoutly to be wished, but where is the evidence? Having read the paper carefully, I see nothing to support this claim. On the contrary, every single point indicates that the situation is seen as positive only in that Jews seek to stick together. That is after all the meaning of cohesiveness and cohesiveness emerges as the main positive quality of the American Jewish community. But such cohesiveness, while indicating that the community wishès to live and not die, does not in any way demonstrate creativity or quality. The description is definitely of a "parve" situation. Intermarriage is on the rise, but the couple tends to identify with the community. Fertility is lower, but still not to the point of worry. Secularization has occurred and religious observance is continually declining but ethnic pride remains strong. This hardly sounds like creativity. The most telling example in the paper is the fact that when discussing Jewish education, the author cites the fact that "parents bring their children to school, have contact with other Jewish parents and with Jewish teachers and other Jewish children...it is clearly what community is all about." Indeed, but it is not what education is all about. The author establishes a good case for the fact that Jewish identity, community and cohesiveness remain, but that is all that he is able to show. The gap between this and claims of great flourishing creativity is wide indeed.

The author also shows that religiously there has been a decline and that more and more Jews tend to be secularized and find their Jewish ties outside of religion. This is undoubtedly true. However, this raises two questions: Can Judaism exist for long outside of Israel without some strong religious base? I have some idea of what secular Judaism means in Israel. I have no idea of what it represents elsewhere, especially in America. Second, for those to whom religion is an indispensable part of Judaism, is Judaism totally secularized or even largely so really important?

Perhaps the problem with the paper is that it has attempted to grasp too much. It should have been content with the claim that American Judaism is not dead or dying, that Jews are trying to remain Jews. The logical step beyond that is not to claim that it is creative and flourishing, but to state that with this as a basis, we must determine what can be done to give it depth and meaning. The community exists, but in what way is it Jewish and in what way should it be Jewish?

As for specific policy recommendations, who can be against bringing more young Jews to Israel? But why not subsidize programs for all, since even the affiliated need reinforcement of their Jewish ties.

Let us be truly appreciative that Professor Goldscheider has laid to rest the myth of the dying American community. But let us face the reality of the American Jewish scene in all of its problematics in order to formulate truly meaningful policies.

The formulation of community guidelines is made more complex by the fact that the community is a pluralistic one which does not share a common view of what Judaism is or what kind of Jew it wants to foster. There are those for whom the religious component is uppermost, and others for whom it is, if not anathema, at least unimportant. Similarly among those who share the religious viewpoint, there are great differences of approach to basic questions of observance and belief. It may therefore be true that the community as such can work only minimally as a group and may have to formulate broad goals which can then be realized by the subgroups within the community according to the principles of each of those groups. This is neither as impossible nor as outrageous as it sounds. It has an excellent precedent in the way in which the American government works through the individual states to accomplish overall goals, each state having different methods and different priorities. In the case of the Jewish community, the division would not be geographic but according to ideology.

What are the broad goals that the community can be said to share and should therefore be willing to foster? I suggest that there are five: 1) Continued existence of the community; 2) Spread of Jewish knowledge; 3) Loyalty to the Jewish people; 4) Interest in and support for Israel; and 5) The ability of the individual to live his life as a Jew in accordance with his beliefs.

For too long the general fund-raising agencies of the community have taken the approach that they should support only those agencies which are open to all and which avoid the issues which divide the community. Thus support for Israel, support for welfare agencies, support for Jewish centers are legitimate concerns, while support for synagogues, rabbinical training schools, religious schools and camps, even day schools are not. The last decade or so has seen some change in this, but not enough. The change has come largely through the fact that enormous Orthodox pressure for the support of day schools led to support for all day schools. It is time for the federations to realize that as long as some formula for parity is arrived at, there is no reason why all educational endeavors of the various arms of the

57

Jewish community should not be supported, from nurseries through seminaries. Each one contributes to all five of the goals which the broad community shares, each in its own way. Only those institutions which do not so contribute, which detract from Judaism or which are not run according to sound principles of education and management should not receive support. Some system of matching funds, again taken from the government model, would be appropriate.

In addition to major funding for synagogues and schools, I would suggest that there should be support for sending each teenager for a summer program to Israel. There is no need to set up new programs--enough exists already--but to provide scholarship aid to enable all youngsters to participate in the program of their choice.

Retreat centers should be established or supported to permit existing agencies, synagogues etc. to hold retreats for families as well as for non-affiliates which would strengthen Jewish identity.

Serious programs for training teachers are virtually nonexistent. Thought should be given to the establishment of such schools by the major movements to be supported by community funds.

While heavily supporting the efforts of individual movements and groups, I believe that it is also important for the community to foster interaction among the groups and opportunities for joint actions and joint mutual respect. Thus conferences on matters of Jewish belief, culture and actions could be sponsored regionally and nationally for leaders and materials prepared and disseminated to the general public which would reflect the plurality of views, but would stress that which is uniquely Jewish.

The publication of a high quality popular magazine of Judaism would also be important, a magazine which would deal with the news of the Jewish World, with issues and ideas and would provide popular educational materials. In short, a magazine for those who wish to be knowledgeable of Jewish life and thought.

The American Jewish community is alive. How well it is living will depend upon its ability to focus upon those areas of concern which will assure continuity and survival by strengthening not only identity but also knowledge and commitment to live according to some interpretation of Judaism meaningful to the individual. The community must then support those groups and institutions which can contribute to these goals.

RITA E. HAUSER
Attorney and Jewish Communal Leader

The discussion relative to emerging leadership in Jewish communities is, to me, the most provocative aspect of the paper in question. It is also the least developed, both conceptually and in its prescriptions for action.

FIRST: the relationship described in the paper is essentially bi-polar: America and Israel. Little mention is made of flourishing, divergent and interesting Jewish communities in Europe and Latin America. These communities have much to contribute to the dynamic of modern Jewish leadership. They have been shunted aside in the past decades because of the dominant and, I believe, imbalanced relationship which has pervaded the Jewish American-Israeli dynamic, discussed further below. As a consequence, the World Jewish Congress, or the American Jewish Committee, to cite but two organizations with strong historic ties to international Jewry, have tended to relate to non-Israeli Jews either with (1) indifference couched in historic nostalgia or (2) with paternalism in the case of Jewish communities in distress. And in the latter instance, American and Israeli Jewish leaders have often clashed in their competition for control over the salvation of the distressed community, e.g., Ethiopian and Soviet Jews.

Accordingly, any new construct for dialogue and interaction in the Jewish world should necessarily include participants from Europe and Latin America on an equal footing with American and Israelis. They will add much to the comprehension of diverse

61

modes of Jewish acculturation, accommodation with power centers, and changing family roles.

SECOND: The paper fails to analyze the unhealthy relationship between American and Israeli Jewish leaders which evolved in the past decades and which, in my opinion, has frozen constructive dialogue between them. The relationship was originally premised on urgent financial need by Israel, an activity which is still dominant despite the fact that private Jewish donations are insignificant in the face of U.S. government aid and subsidies to Israel.

The unwritten premise of this relationship was that Americans contributed and Israelis determined the spending of the money. As long as Israeli policies were congruent with the view of the vast majority of American Jews, this posed no real problem. With the advent of Israeli governments that began to diverge from some of these views, especially in policies concerning absorption of the West Bank and resolution of basic political problems by the use of military power (e.g., the Lebanese invasion), many Americans, and a good number of Israelis, expressed the view that the relationship required more than just fund-raising. It required an activist interchange, including mutual critiques, an open assessment of limitations of support and, in general, a frank give-and-take arrangement. This has not yet occurred, and the younger leaders in both America and Israel who have promoted this change, have been thwarted, sometimes brutally, by the older generation of leaders whose experiences and insecurities preclude such an open interaction.

This change is inevitable. Programs should be oriented toward promoting its smooth advent, facilitating an honest exchange of views on a basis of equality. As stated earlier, Jewish leaders of other communities have a rightful place in this relationship. Mutual criticism and constructive analysis are at the heart of a flourishing entente which now should prevail in the Jewish secular world. University exchanges, seminars, writings, inter-connections of all sorts underlie the type of constructive change described above.

It is time world Jewry acknowledges the reality, not just the existence, of a Jewish State. By that, I mean the fact that this State, like any other, is not a utopia, but a real place, replete with problems in every domain of life. Similarly, Israeli leaders need finally to acknowledge the reality of the Diaspora, and accept the fact of multiple centers of Jewish life in which Jews deal with daily problems totally independent of Israel and its concerns.

An era is ending, indeed, probably already ended, with the maturation of Israel following its 1967 military victory. Yet Jewish organized life is still dominated by people grounded in the experiences of the preceding decades, and who still fear Israel's momentary demise. Alas, some of the younger leaders have adopted the counterface of this fear, and they pursue an aggressive stance in which the only issue that seems to matter is Israel's military power. Relating to the complex phenomenon that is Israel, in more than military terms, has eluded many of these younger leaders. Their politics have alienated a large group of Jewish people who would like to be involved in matters which deal with other concerns, particularly humanitarian and social, and not necessarily limited to Jewish welfare.

Many American Jews remain deeply concerned about a wide range of issues confronting them in the United States. So do French Jews as to France, or Argentinian Jews as to Argentina. Israeli leaders, on the whole, are ignorant of or dismiss these issues as secondary to Israel and its concerns. I strongly believe the time is ripe for a world Jewish agenda, in which the life of all Jewish communities is relevant. There is need for policies and programs to promote leadership that can surpass the limitations of the donor-donee relationship which has polarized Jewish organizational life since the establishment of the State of Israel.

HAROLD S. HIMMELFARB
Ohio State University

Calvin Goldscheider has presented us with an important corrective to the gloom and doom predictions about the future of the American Jewish community so prevalent among Jewish leadership today. Many persons have been citing social science evidence to show that the future of the American Jewish community, both in quantity and quality, is bleak, and predictions of the future have reached near hysterical proportions. Yet, I might add, hardly anyone in the American Jewish community who cites such statistics, really believes that the crisis is imminent. Otherwise, I presume, rational people would act on their beliefs and the *aliyah* (immigration to Israel) rate among the doomsayers, at least, would be substantial. Since it is not, we can surmise that the statistics are used to exhort Jews back to the fold and to get them more involved in more active and committed ways.

In contrast, Professor Goldscheider believes that the situation of American Jewry is exactly opposite to the thrust of the assimilation-disappearance position. "...It is neither diminishing demographically nor weakening Jewishly. It is...becoming more Jewish, stronger...(and is) entering a period of flourishing and creative development..." Moreover, he argues that this view is "not based on ideology, optimism, or perspective on whether the glass is half-full or half-empty. It is an interpretation of new social scientific evidence..."

Presumably, then, once we all see the evidence, we can agree. Unfortunately, neither the evidence, nor its interpretation is

65

consistent, and social scientists, who should be able to view the facts with dispassion and neutrality, have hardly reached a consensus about them. Indeed, I believe that consensus will only come from moderation. Both positions, that of the doomsayers and that of flourishers, are overstated. There are many signs of individual assimilation and weakness in the community, but clearly American Jewry is not about to disappear soon or diminish in great proportions; not even in the next 90 years, as some bi-centennial predictions asserted about the tri-centennial in America. There are also many signs of strength, particularly at the institutional level, and these need to be recognized too. Clearly, if all was well, we would not need papers on how to ameliorate the problems! Leave well enough alone!

The following comments will first discuss the evidence to which Professor Goldscheider refers and its implications, and, second, the policies he recommends.

THE EVIDENCE

Family Size

For some time, it has been common knowledge in the Jewish community that American Jews have fewer children than other Americans; as the fertility rate has dropped among Americans generally to below 2.1 children, which is replacement level, it has dropped to well below replacement level among Jews. Thus, it was assumed if young Americans will have a completed fertility of around 1.8, Jewish fertility will probably be around 1.5.

Professor Goldscheider argues correctly that the timing of childbearing has undergone dramatic change. Therefore, one cannot predict what total fertility will be from the lower level of fertility among younger Jewish women compared to the fertility of older women when they were young. Although Jewish women are postponing childbearing until their late 20s and early thirties, there is still sufficient time for them to have an average of two children. If one looks at the number of children expected, he argues, Jewish women will be well within replacement level. Therefore, the American Jewish population is not in decline.

However, even stable population growth (replacement) can have some negative consequences while the rest of the population

66

is growing. An analysis of National Opinion Research Center data collected between 1972 and 1983 by Tom Smith, showed that Jews born prior to 1907 constituted 3.1 percent of the American population, but those born between 1958 and 1965 constituted only 0.8 percent of the American population. I agree with Professor Goldscheider, that size has never been the main source of Jewish strength or influence in this country. However, I am not sure that declining to less than 1 percent of the population will not have some effect on their ability to wield political influence. Moreover, it is not clear that these figures or proportions reflect stable Jewish population size, rather than actual numerical decline. The latter would affect Jewish institutions at all levels.

The truth is that there is no good way to know what future fertility will be, particularly since we are in a period of drastic timing changes. It is also true that there is considerable disagreement among demographers whether birth expectations are better predictors of completed births than period estimates of different age cohorts. Nevertheless, it is true that birth expectations have given reasonably good estimates of completed fertility for moderate range time-spans of 5 to 10 years. We do not know how well they predict completed life-time fertility. Even if we accept expectation data as accurate, we can voice some reservations. For example, Goldscheider and Kobrin's analysis of data from the High School Class of 1972 shows that Jewish females on the average expect about 1.9 children. If we look at their data, the National Survey of Family Growth, and adjust for the tendency of such data to overestimate actual births by 10 percent to 15 percent, we are left with a total of expected births for Jewish women of about 1.8. Thus, while it is true that expectation figures, if realized, do not foretell the rapid decline predicted by averages of 1.5 children, they still indicate fertility below replacement level.

Thus, it seems that there *is* a population size problem, even if not as severe as some have estimated. Also, it is important to note that there are segments of the American Jewish population (primarily among the Orthodox and, especially, the Hassidic communities), where Jewish population growth is well beyond replacement. Therefore, there is not a question of Jews disappearing from the American scene, but there is the possibility of reduced numbers, along with substantial changes in the community's social and religious character, including its nationalistic orientations toward America and toward Israel.

67

If we acknowledge that there is a population size problem due to declining fertility, the real question for policy makers is whether anything can be done about it. While governments in various countries have been somewhat successful in instituting policies to reduce births, few have been successful in instituting policies which increase births. It has been tried a number of times. Certainly, the organized American Jewish community has many fewer and compelling incentives to offer to encourage positive population growth than do political states. Thus, one cannot be optimistic that there is much that can be done about the problem or that something ought to be tried.

On the other hand, the fact that there are segments of the population that have positive population growth rooted in ideological factors and normative climates that encourage larger families, does indicate that there might be some ways to improve the situation, at least a little. Thus, I would suggest that (a) the problem should not be removed from the Jewish community's agenda, and (b) that it should continue to be discussed in synagogues, schools, and communal organizations, in order to create an ideological imperative for larger families. In fact, all that needs to be changed is the notion that the most desirable number of children is two, and increase it to three. An increase of one child per family on the average would move the community into positive rather than negative population growth. (c) To the extent that structural barriers within Jewish institutions can be removed in order to increase fertility it ought to be tried, e.g., free Jewish school tuition for all children in a family beyond the first two. (d) To the extent that the organized community can influence the general societal climate about children, as advocates of pro-family legislation and part-time work arrangements, Jews ought to get involved. (e) Finally, because most countries which have tried, have failed in their attempts to increase population size, I would not make policy intervention in this sphere of Jewish community problems a top organizational priority, nor would I spend large sums of money annually on programs whose primary purpose is to increase Jewish population growth. Quiet "moral persuasion" would probably be the best policy at this time.

Intermarriage

The evidence on intermarriage is more clear to me that the evidence on population, and it is also much less positive than Goldscheider suggests. Intermarried couples and families

68

generally are less involved with all forms of Jewish identification than families where both spouses were born Jewish. However, where the non-Jewish spouse has converted to Judaism, the couple is often more Jewish involved than typical third generation American Jewishly-born couples. Ironically, however, the greater involvement is usually restricted to the religious spheres of Jewish identification, and does not extend to the ethnic spheres (e.g., Jewish organizational participation)--the main way that American Jews exhibit their Jewish identification. Since conversions to Judaism only take place in about one-quarter of intermarriages, the net effect of intermarriage *is* a loss to the Jewish people, both in terms of numbers and quality of Jewish life. However, since 15 percent to 25 percent of Jewish couples where both spouses are born Jewish have little to no involvement in Jewish life, the net loss due to intermarriage is not as great as the intermarriage figures themselves. That is, some of those who intermarry, would have had little Jewish involvement even if they married another Jew. The estimates of net loss that I have seen or calculated from various studies range between 2 percent and 15 percent, depending on the criterion of Jewish definition of involvement that is used to determine a loss (e.g., Do both spouses consider themselves Jewish? Do they plan to raise the children as Jews? Do they expect to send the children to a Jewish school?) These estimates do not adjust for the lower fertility rates among intermarried couples compared to Jewishly-born couples, which would increase the estimate of net loss.

These figures are far different from those that consider every intermarriage as a loss to the Jewish people. It seems that it is the latter estimate to which Professor Goldscheider is reacting. Nevertheless, intermarriage results in a net loss to the Jewish community and it is misleading to suggest otherwise. In fact, I find it quite contradictory to argue that intermarriage is not a problem for the Jewish people and then label the intermarried as "marginal" Jews for whom programs need to be developed. If they are more "marginal" than other Jews, then they are a problem.

Again, the question for policymakers is whether anything can be done about intermarriage; and, again the answer is: "probably not much." I certainly agree with Professor Goldscheider that intermarriage, for most Jews, does not derive from a desire to assimilate. In most cases, it is a normal consequence of increased interaction and socializing with non-Jews. Intermarriage will be reduced only when young Jews are sufficiently involved in Jewish life that the sub-cultural differences between them and their potential non-Jewish mates are great enough to reduce their mutual attraction for marital purposes. No simple solution! Indeed it can be argued that certain conditions which might bring this about, such as various forms of isolation from society-at-large, might have other consequences that are unacceptable. Actually short of reducing intermarriage, as Professor Goldscheider suggests, greater efforts have to be made to attract the non-Jewish spouse to Judaism, or, at least, create enough receptivity to Jews and Jewish culture that the children will be raised Jewishly. Since the evidence on Jewish identification of intermarried families where the non-Jewish spouse has converted to Judaism is quite positive, more research needs to be done on the conversion process itself, to understand what aspects are most effective and, of course, how it interacts with background factors in the marital partners' lives.

Perhaps social science evidence can help enlighten Halachic criteria for conversion which obviously have ramifications of international and long-term proportions, and ultimately will affect the unity of the Jewish people. One thing seems fairly clear from the evidence available now (although more direct evidence would still be welcome); the traditional practice of discouraging conversion as a way of testing personal conviction probably has more long-term negative consequences for the results of potential intermarriage than an opposite approach. Few Jews are likely to be deterred from marriage by their partner's decision not to convert, and the non-Jewish partners are probably less likely to be supportive of a Jewish life-style in the home than if they had converted.

Mobility

Professor Goldscheider is correct that the long-term effects of high Jewish mobility are few. That is, there does seem to be some disruptive effect on Jewish affiliation for newcomers to communities, but much of it is due more to the fact that those who move around are younger and often less affiliated anyhow. Of course, those who continue to move may have long-term disaffiliation rates, but that is not the average pattern.

Of more concern, is the dispersal of Jews throughout the peripheral areas of large urban communities. The evidence

70

indicates that generally Jews seek to live among other Jews, and once Jewishly sparse suburbs often become fairly Jewishly concentrated areas. However, I suspect that the new areas remain less Jewishly concentrated than the old neighborhoods of several decades ago, particularly in areas other than the east coast. Such dispersal is costly in terms of Jewish institutional life, and the physical facilities, human resources, and transportation services needed for active participation in Jewish institutions. From a policy viewpoint, there is much room for Jewish organizations to be more active in promoting Jewish neighborhood concentration and stability, and the creation of affordable and attractive housing for younger Jewish families in neighborhoods of current Jewish concentration where residential housing tends to be very expensive. There are already some models of successful intervention in this regard.

Occupational Patterns

The notion that growing education, occupational, and social class similarities among American Jews is a source of ethnic cohesion is an innovative and intriguing idea, and I anxiously await the data that support it. Frankly, I am skeptical that such a causal relationship exists. It seems more likely to me that the increased proportion of salaried professionals among Jews will necessitate increased contacts with non-Jews, and also necessitate professional referrals and interactions that are based more purely on professional criteria than was true years ago when people preferred to deal-with and refer-to *landsmen*. Moreover, the personal investment and lengthy socialization in preparation for careers these days probably creates a greater tendency than in previous generations for persons to concentrate their informal and personal relationships among work associates rather than fellow ethnics. That is not to say, that Jews do not maintain primarily Jewish friendships, but that their changed occupational characteristics probably lessen rather than heighten this trend.

Institutional Strength

Despite these patterns of individual assimilation and attrition just described, I agree that there is indeed much strength in the American Jewish community today. The community is more well organized and coordinated, more sophisticatedly and efficiently run, and more financially well-off than ever before. Many of our social service agencies can be national models for similar institutions. The Israel political lobby is one of the most effective lobbies in the country. The ability of the Jewish community to mobilize human, economic and political resources is truly great and amazing, particularly when one realizes that ultimately the organization of the community is highly decentralized and individual participation is voluntary.

This strength persists, and probably is even growing, despite signs of numerical attrition. Whether, over the long run, institutional strength will continue to persist in the context of individual attrition is questionable; however, so is the issue of continued attrition. There is evidence from a few studies that assimilatory patterns will stabilize by the fourth generation, albeit at low levels of Jewish involvement.

POLICIES

The "Policy Orientations, Targets and Goals" that Professor Goldscheider lists seem to be very much on target and well-reasoned. Similarly, the "Arenas for Policy Development" outline an appropriate agenda for action among a wide range of constituencies. Again, it is somewhat paradoxical, that those whom he previously argued were not Jewishly impaired or marginal, are later targeted for programmatic aid, i.e., the intermarried and migrants.

I would add to this agenda the need for spiritual revitalization (cultural and religious) among the mainstream of Jews. That is, more has to be done to make programs exciting and compelling, not just for marginal Jews, but for those who belong to synagogues and Jewish organizations, but get very little enhancement of their Jewish identities out of it. After all, programs are likely to be more successful with those who have felt a need to affiliate than with those who have to be attracted through "outreach." Families with children of Jewish school age need to be worked with so as to break the cycle of increasing generational attrition.

While one might argue that these are the persons for whom existing institutions already target their programs, I would argue that not enough is being done to provide quality programming. Community planning and coordination can provide resources, which transcend the means and capabilities of individual congregations, schools or organizational chapters. Mass media programming of high quality and artistry can be disseminated nationally. They give greater visibility and legitimacy to Jewish cultural activities. Organizationally, I believe that there is greater need for federations and synagogues to work together on some of these programs, and to disabuse ourselves of the notion that denominationally sponsored programs by definition do not serve a community-wide function. There is a need to fund and disseminate programs of excellence wherever they originate, and there is need to establish sound bases for evaluating excellence.

A few comments in regard to the specific policies or programs recommended by Professor Goldscheider:

a) Summer programs in Israel have proven to be very positive experiences for Jewish teenagers. I do not believe that the phenomenon is sufficiently widespread among the general Jewish teenage populace that unaffiliated teenagers need to be targeted as a top priority. Thus, there should be greater efforts to include such an experience as part of regular Jewish school or other teenage programming. Jewish overnight summer camping should run a close second to this in terms of efforts exerted to make it as universal as attending a Jewish school. I would not offer free summer trips to anyone, whether affiliated or not. People who pay for advice are more likely to accept it than those who do not. People who pay for educational programs are more likely to take them seriously than those who do not. Programs need to be made affordable through subsidization and scholarships, but some individual effort also needs to be made if the program's goals are to be achieved. One other point on this matter: Studies show that the duration of impact of camping and Israel programs depends considerably on the availability of follow-up programs back home to reinforce what was gained while away. This aspect needs greater implementation.

b) There is some evidence that the college-age group could very possibly be the most important group for whom to target programs. They have probably been the most neglected of all groups with regard to Jewish programming, and they are certainly one of the most difficult groups to attract to such programming. However, I am doubtful whether "modern Jewish studies" will be their biggest "turn-on." More likely, informal, experimental type programming will attract a greater number of students. There is a need to convene high level groups of Hillel directors, professors, Jewish student leaders and others involved in Jewish campus activities to exchange ideas and recommendations about how to program for the group. College is probably a more universal experience among Jewish students than Hebrew school. Ways should be found to successfully program for this large group.

c) The issues raised by Professor Goldscheider regarding the growing cultural gap between Israeli leaders and American leaders is very insightful. His analysis of educational, gender and religious differences are astute and raise great concerns. The need for cultural exchanges among young leaders from both countries would seem self-evident, although the programmatic solution is not. The problem in the religious sphere is compounded in both countries by the lack of communication and interchange between the Orthodox rabbinate and others. There is also a growing gap between the recognized Orthodox leadership in Israel, surrounding the chief rabbinate and the Mizrachi-type rabbinical leaders, and the leadership that is most recognized by Orthodox rabbis in America, which surrounds the Aguda and right-wing Orthodox *yeshivot*. Thus, in addition to getting Israeli leaders to exchange ideas with American leaders, there is also a great need to get Orthodox rabbis in both countries to exchange ideas with other Orthodox and non-Orthodox rabbis. How to begin to implement the latter, completely escapes me. Perhaps, it would be easier to work on bringing the Messiah!

Calvin Goldscheider has done us all a great favor by stimulating our minds to draw policy implications from research evidence. It is a difficult exercise, but like all exercises it should get easier the more we continue to do it.

RICHARD G. HIRSCH
World Union for Progressive Judaism

"Israel among the nations is like the heart amidst the organs of the body; it is at one and the same time the most sick and the most healthy of them" (Kuzari II:36). After reading Calvin Goldscheider's paper, Judah Halevi's statement of the 12th century seems even more poignant. The doctor has taken the pulse of American Jewry and has given his diagnosis: We are in good health. "The total community picture appears robust." Modernization does not lead to assimilation. "The American Jewish community is a powerful and cohesive community. It has strong anchors of social, religious, and family life; it is neither diminishing demographically nor weakening Jewishly"...We are "entering a period of flourishing and creative development" rather "than one reflecting the final gasps of a declining, weakening struggling to survive remnant."

Not being a social scientist, I have no way of evaluating the statistics which provide the data base for Professor Goldscheider's revisionist theory. As a rabbi, I believe that the unquenchable passion for survival is a prime motivating factor in Jewish life. Our key vitamin is hope, hope for the future, hope in the future, hope *Lamrot Hakol*, hope despite everything, despite all the obstacles. If Professor Goldscheider's findings inject new hope, new insights, new directions for effective Jewish living, then they represent an important contribution.

However, I cannot help but feel that, to continue Yehudah Halevi's metaphor, we are also sick, and that Professor

Goldscheider minimizes the symptoms of the illness. Unless the doctors recognize the nature of the illness, we cannot prescribe the proper care for our patient, the American Jewish community. Why are we "at one and the same time the most sick and the most healthy of them?" Because American Jewry tries to live in two worlds. The emancipation of the Jew continues to confront us with its inherent dilemma. How do we reconcile the tension between the aspiration for integration and the passion for Jewish survival? How do we become a part of and still remain apart from American society? How do we respond affirmatively to modernity without diluting or destroying the distinctive character of the Jewish people? In short, how do we share fully in the American dream while preventing it from becoming a Jewish nightmare?

There are among us those who would give extreme answers to the perpetual dilemma--integration or survival? Among the extreme survivalists are the advocates of classical Zionism who state forthrightly that there is no future in the Diaspora, and that Jews must remove themselves from the seduction of America and reestablish Jewish sovereignity in a Jewish state. Another example of extreme survivalists are the ultra-Orthodox Hassidic groups who establish insulated Jewish communities, separated both from the outside secular world and from the larger Jewish community. On the other end of the spectrum are the extreme integrationists, the assimilationists, those who are indifferent to Jewish survival, and who, for all practical purposes are prepared to lose their identity as Jews. Among the extreme integrationists are those who, while retaining Jewish identity, would so radically transform the Jewish character as to call into question the essence of survival. Within this latter category are classic Reform Jews who organized the American Council for Judaism and others who would contract Jewishness into a faith by eliminating the peoplehood dimensions. However, the vast majority of American Jews will not put themselves in the category of either extreme. Those who want to retain their Jewish identity are in search of a synthesis between integration and survival. In the search for a synthesis, the existence of many different and even conflicting ideologies and programs is not only inevitable, but also salutary. The American Jewish community is grounded in voluntarism. Because no Jew is forced to join, contribute, or be active, every Jew is a legitimate target audience. In the free market of America, every organization, institution and movement is encouraged to compete for the heart, the mind, the body, and the pocketbook of American Jews. Given the American milieu, a multiplicity of approaches serves a positive purpose.

Social scientists like Dr. Goldscheider perform a useful and vital function. They can analyze attitudes and practices. They can shatter preconceptions and stereotypes. They can bring to bear new insights and point to new policy directions. But scientific objectivity invariably gives way to subjectivity. Here is where Professor Goldscheider's paper must be put into perspective. His facts cannot be evaluated in a vacuum. His presentation is predicated on his own subjective attitudes. He makes, or at least implies, value judgments, and once we enter the sphere of value judgment, the premises and conclusions must be tested in the crucible of conflicting Jewish experiences and purposes.

We Jews are a people of firm convictions. *Ichpat Li,* "I care deeply" is a key phrase in the contemporary Hebrew vocabulary. We care deeply about the issues of Jewish life. Take as an example three areas of value judgment dealt with by Dr. Goldscheider. The first is intermarriage. Goldscheider contends that "intermarriage in the United States in the 1970s and 1980s is likely to be a qualitative and quantitative gain." "Intermarriage needs to be understood less as a threat to Jewish continuity and more as a challenge for Jewish communal policies." To be sure, in an open society, some degree of intermarriage is inevitable. If an increasing number of Jews are marrying non-Jews, then how vital it is for us to make every effort to draw the non-Jewish spouse into the Jewish fold and to foster a relationship which will result in conversion to Judaism before or after the wedding. How encouraging it is to learn that with increasing frequency the intermarried couples, even without conversion, prefer identifying with the Jewish community and raising their children as Jews.

But the premise that intermarriage represents a "gain" and is not a "threat to Jewish continuity," is a value judgment I find totally unacceptable. Should not our ideal objective be that every Jew should marry another Jew? If so, how can we afford to remove the stigma against intermarriage? Should we not expend great efforts to formulate policies and institute programs to prevent intermarriage? If, as Goldscheider contends, the family is a central focus of Jewish cohesion, then is not the Jewish character of the extended family deleteriously affected when either the husband or wife's family is not Jewish? In sum, in relating to intermarriage, we must zealously differentiate between making the best of a bad situation *ex post facto* and *ab initio* forsaking the

77

legitimate and vital expectation of Jewish parents and the Jewish community that Jews should marry Jews.

A second value judgment relates to Goldscheider's call for symmetry in Israel-American relations. The word *symmetry* is synonymous with *equality* or *parity*. From the context of statements in several places in the article, Goldscheider would appear to adopt the ideology which presumes that there are two equal foci of Jewish life, America and Israel. The theory that America is another Babylon continues to generate debate, at least within Zionist circles. I am an ardent advocate of greater direct participation and involvement of American Jews in Israel, including criticism of Israel by American Jews. All too many Israelis understate the achievements of American Jewry and its potential for creative survival. I agree with almost all of Goldscheider's analysis of the differences between Israeli and American Jewry and the necessity of developing reciprocal programs to bridge the gaps.

Nevertheless, I would never use the word *symmetry* or *parity* to describe the ideal relationship. My argument with Goldscheider is more than semantic. It is ideological. Nowhere in his policy orientations, targets, and goals is there reference to the American Jewish obligation to foster Aliyah. Is this because there appears to be little hope for any significant Aliyah? Or because in Goldscheider's view Aliyah is not a priority of American Jewry? I dare say that if a poll were to be taken of American Jewish leadership, the majority would contend that from the perspective of Jewish survival, the key question is not *where* Jews live, but *how* Jews live. Not so with the majority of Israeli Zionists. From the perspective of Israelis, the Jewish state must have a significant majority of Jews. Given the current demographic patterns in the Arab and Jewish populations and the current rate of *Aliyah* and *Yeridah*, within a generation Jews may be a minority in the borders of Eretz Yisrael. Without Aliyah, Israel will never have the critical mass essential to sustaining a state Jewish in character as well as in name. Moreover, Israel cannot be the spiritual center of the Jewish people if only 20 percent of world Jewry lives in the center and 80 percent lives in the Diaspora.

When Zionists refer in the Jerusalem Program to the "centrality of the State of Israel" there is a clear value judgment that the upbuilding of Zion is the central task of the Jewish people today. This does not mean that the individual Jew living in Israel is in any way superior to or more virtuous than the individual Jew in the United States. Nor does it mean that the 3,000,000 strong Jewish community of Israel is better than the 3,000,000 strong Jewish community of New York, or the 6,000,000 strong Jewish community of America. It does mean that from the perspective of Jewish survival, a Jew living in Israel by his very presence does more than anywhere else to preserve the collectivity called the Jewish people. Today, following the Holocaust, and the establishment of the State, it is difficult to project the continued creative survival of the Jewish people without a strong, dynamic Jewish state.

From this perspective, there is no symmetry and there can be no parity. In America, every Jew has an option on the extent to which he wants to take part in the task of preserving the Jewish people. In Israel, every Jew is obligated to perform the national task of preserving the Jewish people. In America, Jewishness is a private matter, expressed through home, synagogue and Jewish community. In Israel, the private and public sectors of Jewish life are integrated and inseparable.

At stake here is a question of Jewish priorities. As an individual, every Jew has a right to live wherever he wants. But as a community, a major priority of American Jewry has to be the development of action programs leading to Aliyah and the numerical strengthening of the Jewish state.

A third value judgment made by Goldscheider relates to the role of religion as a preservation force. He claims that "the evidence available confirms unambiguously declining religiosity and ritual practice among the younger generations. There seems to be little doubt about the growing secularization of American Jews." I have never accepted facile delineations made either in Israel or in the United States between "religious" and "secular". Just because an activity in a synagogue is sandwiched between an opening invocation and a closing benediction, it does not mean that the experience is religious. Or, conversely, that an experience in a so-called secular environment cannot be spiritually uplifting. The Bible describes us as a "holy people." The genius of Judaism is its capacity to find holiness in everyday events. Similarly with the delineation between "ethnicity" and "religion." When no Jew in Israel would ever think of driving a car on Yom Kippur, is that evidence of religiousness, ethnicity or national consciousness, or a combination of all? In essence, it is the inseparable mixture of faith, people, and culture which distinguishes the Jewish character from most other civilizations.

My experience with American Jews, particularly among younger generations, gives evidence that there is a profound search for Jewish roots, for Jewish knowledge and Jewish experiences. To attempt to categorize the search into pre-set molds marked "religious", "secular", or "ethnic" is unproductive. Every search for Jewish experiences should be encouraged and facilitated.

I endorse Goldscheider's call to provide opportunities for Jews to "interact." But what is the "action" which is the basis for "interaction?" I would suggest that the most effective "interaction" is predicated on shared "actions" with fellow Jews which enrich Jewish knowledge and commitment. Being Jewish has to involve more than just having Jewish family, friends, and business associates. Jewish action and interaction should serve to attach Jews to the eternal values and expressions associated with Jewishness. Ultimately, significant portions of these values and expressions are rooted in life-cycle events, the Sabbath, holidays and other Jewish observances associated with the synagogue and the home. Therefore, policies which do not aspire to some manifestation of Jewish religious way of life are not likely to be enduring.

Which leads me to an analysis of Goldscheider's policy recommendations. In and of themselves, they are all good ideas and could make splendid contributions to Jewish continuity. Here and there I would quibble about some of the specifics (for example, whereas trips to Israel should be subsidized, both from the psychological and fiscal points of view participants should bear part of the burden). However, Goldscheider's recommendations raise questions of priority, and priority in turn is predicated on available resources. The proliferation of courses in Jewish studies at universities reflects a growing interest in and pride of the Jewish heritage. But all too often there is a gap between the mind and the soul. Our tradition has a radical statement: "He who learns without doing, it is preferable if he had not been born" (Talmud Yerushalmi, Shabbat Aleph, Bet). The most effective learning must lead to doing. Judaism must be "caught" as well as taught. My own priority, therefore, is for programs which lead to some form of continuous personal commitment and action.

I agree that Israel offers a splendid framework for Jewish education and identification. An effective Israel experience can provide an enduring injection in Judaism, a long-lasting immunization against assimilation. By coincidence, I am the Israel chairman of a new project of the Jewish Education Committee of the Jewish Agency called *The Israel Experience*. The project has engaged a highly professional research team of social scientists to make an inventory of all existing programs in Israel. The committee will shortly recommend ways to increase significantly the numbers of persons who have an *Israel Experience* and to recommend ways of making these programs more effective. It will also recommend new and innovative pilot projects, in which Goldscheider's suggestions could well be included.

Much stress has to be placed in devising programs where Israeli and Diaspora Jewry meet and get to know each other. A common complaint of participants in existing Israel programs is that they have little contact with Israeli peers. Many overseas students spend a year at an Israeli university without establishing a personal relationship with even one Israeli. Interaction is essential both to bridge the differences and to forge personal relationships between Israeli and Diaspora Jews.

Another vital bond which leads to cohesion is the Hebrew language. We tend to think of language as a vehicle for the communication of thoughts and values. But for the modern Jew, knowledge of Hebrew is a value in and of itself. The Hebrew language has become the symbol of a renewed Jewish people and a renascent Jewish culture. The revivification of the Hebrew language, unspoken for more than 2,000 years, represents a modern miracle. As much as the Jew has revived Hebrew, Hebrew has revived the Jewish people. I urge, as an educational objective, that modern Hebrew become a second language for Diaspora Jewry. If we were to adopt this educational objective as a basic policy of American Jewry, we would have to create a vast and costly system of ulpanim, schools and camps in the Diaspora, provide more extended learning experiences in Israel, as well as on-going experiences at all levels in Jewish communities and homes around the world. Is this program far-fetched? Not as far-fetched as when Eliezer Ben Yehuda first proposed Hebrew as the language of the Jewish state less than one hundred years ago. Is it controversial? Yes, because the very process of formulating the objective would force us to rethink the nature of our existence in the Diaspora. Is it worth it? Yes, because the Hebrew language can serve as the bridge between the soul and the soil of *Am Yisrael*. For the sake of Jewish continuity we need sturdy bridges to our heritage and to our fellow Jews.

One final word. The research and policy proposals of Professor Goldscheider, and of the commentators who responded, should not be left to gather dust. Jewish think tanks have their place. But in this space age, laboratory research should lead to lift-off. The perpetuation of the Jewish people requires a radical rocket-like thrust into the future. Who makes policy and who implements policy for American Jewry? These are prerequisite questions which must be addressed. It is my suggestion that these kinds of discussion quickly be placed on the agenda of major instrumentalities in the Jewish world, such as the Jewish Agency, World Zionist Organization, the Council of Jewish Federations, the major religious movements and large private foundations, for serious coordinated policy planning. With confidence in our capacity, vitality and eternity, let us take the words of Jeremiah as our motto, "There is hope for they future, saith the Lord" (Jeremiah 31:17).

WOLFE KELMAN
The Rabbinical Assembly

How a community or society views itself is not necessarily related to social or economic realities. Jimmy Carter gazed into the rose garden and saw a country afflicted by widespread malaise and found himself resoundingly defeated for reelection with a legacy of incompetence which is not entirely deserved. A successor looked at his cue cards, proclaimed an America standing tall and it did not take too long for the mood and self-portrait of America to undergo a radical revision.

In Israel-American relations, it was not so long ago that most Israelis stood tall and viewed themselves as the last best hope and refuge of Jews living in oppressed societies as well as those who may think they are living in free societies and do not realize how fragile their roots are. Today, most Israelis look to the American government and the American Jewish community as the ultimate guarantor of Israeli's political independence, military superiority over its neighbors, and for avoiding economic bankruptcy.

It was not too long ago that books, articles and sermons about the fate of the American Jews resounded with prophecies of doom and decline, apathy and assimilation, zero or minus population growth. In the last few years, a new assertive self-confidence has begun to emerge based in part on the aftermath of the war in Lebanon, in part on the Reagan mood and mode and the emergence of a group of demographers and sociologists who deal with facts and studies rather than projections and fantasies. It is perhaps no accident that beginning with the American Jewish

83

Year Book with studies by Goldscheider, Goldstein, and Cohen, books are beginning to appear for more general consumption which reflect this mood of repudiating the projections of decline and reaffirming what Goldscheider asserts that "It is much more appropriate to describe the potential future of the American Jewish community as one entering a period of flourishing and creative development than one reflecting the final gasps of a declining, weakening, struggle to survive....based on new, detailed social scientific evidence and a reanalysis of historical and comparative materials on Jews and other ethnic groups in the United States.... *modernization does not lead to assimilation...*"

I was not surprised to hear that for the first time, the General Assembly of the Jewish Federation of Welfare Funds will have an overall theme, "North American Jewry Comes of Age." This Assembly convened shortly after the appearance of Charles Silberman's new volume, which is a repudiation of the thesis that American Jewry is an ever dying and endangered species.

It is no secret that I have been a lone wolf crying in the wilderness for several decades that the *gevalt* syndrome does not reflect the emerging American Jewish community. The thesis about the good old days as compared to the present bleak ones and future dire ones is reminiscent of the story told about the editor of *Punch* magazine who was alleged to have said that *"Punch magazine is not what it used to be and what's more, it never was."*

I was in a distinct minority in an atmosphere where predictions of a catastrophic intermarriage rate and the decline of the American Jewish community were dominant. I still recall how I was almost physically abused when more than fifteen years ago at a public Plenary session of the World Jewish Congress, I spoke of the radical difference in the nature of intermarriage and that it might even produce a net gain for the Jewish people. I was accused of encouraging intermarriage to which I responded that people are not seduced by books, to paraphrase Jimmy Walker, nor intermarriages encouraged by slogans.

In recent years, credible evidence has become available concerning the number of Jews by choice who have adopted Judaism either for marriage or other reasons. It is estimated that in the past ten years, approximately one hundred thousand new Jews by choice have been added to the Jewish population of the

United States. In the years to come, this pool will provide at least an equal if not larger number of additions to the Jewish community. Personal experience and the results of other studies also confirm that a substantial number of these new Jews have developed strong attachments and commitments to Jewish faith and religion, many of them being active synagogue members, attending daily worship services and an increasing number have been ordained as rabbis in all the denominations. The same research also reveals that these Jews by choice who have a strong attachment to the Jewish religion have a very vague or marginal attachment to the Jewish people and the fate and destiny in the land of Israel. I believe that increasing attention will have to be paid by the organized Jewish community to strengthen and deepen the ties of these Jews by choice to the Jewish people which seems to come more naturally to people who are born as Jews even in a marginal Jewish home.

Resources will have to be allocated to bring these people to Israel as individuals or as families for at least one month where they can be immersed in Jewish studies and encounters with the land and people of Israel. Perhaps there should even be one or more well-located Ulpanim with a staff of instructors and guides especially sensitive to strengthening the Jewish feeling and commitment of Jews by choice.

I would point to the fact that more people were involved in the full-time study of Torah from nursery through post-graduate Kollel and other post-graduate studies than ever before in our history, and encountered disdain or name calling about my naive optimism.

It is encouraging to find that what had been a distinct minority voice has now been vindicated by credible scholars like Professors Steve Cohen and Calvin Goldscheider as well as in the volume "A Certain People" by Charles Silberman. I need hardly add that I basically concur with Goldscheider's analysis, but wish to make a few additional observations.

As has been noted by others, simple truths are either/or and more profound truths are either and/or. Thus, it is fair to say that the American Jewish community is both the most thoroughly organized and most centralized of any of our contemporary communities. At the same time, it is also true that less than 50 percent of the known Jewish population in the United States is affiliated with any synagogue or other national Jewish organization and less than 50 percent contributed to the United Jewish Appeal, with the percentage decreasing with the size of the community. The organized Jewish community will have to address itself much more vigorously to devising programs for reaching these unaffiliated or marginal Jews to whom the present synagogal and organizational structure has no appeal and evokes no automatic loyalty.

It would be important to ascertain how much the American Jewish community presently spends on Jewish activities both here and abroad. The organized Federations and Welfare Funds raise approximately six or seven hundred million dollars annually, approximately half of which is retained for domestic purposes for the support of Federation sponsored institutions and national organizations and the remainder sent to Israel through the United Jewish Appeal. About another three to four hundred million dollars is raised directly by institutions in Israel ranging from the Hebrew University to other institutions of higher learning to the smaller institutions and charismatic individuals who collect substantial funds for various educational and religious purposes in Israel.

It has been estimated that anywhere from two to five billion dollars is spent by American Jews for specific Jewish purposes, depending on how that is defined, from synagogues, day schools, summer camps, up to and including kosher catering institutions, etc. It would be important to have more accurate data on how much the American Jewish community spends on Jewish needs here and abroad, whether additional funds can be raised, from what sources and for what purposes they might be allocated, especially for reaching the unaffiliated.

It is also true that most of the existing structures, ideologies and institutions pre-date World War II and some pre-date World War I. Thus, virtually none of the existing major institutions or ideologies have arisen in response to what are undoubtedly the two major events of the 20th century, the Holocaust and the State of Israel.

At the same time, these very same institutions are trying to grapple with a constituency, the majority of whom are third and fourth generation native born Americans, a growing number of whom have matured in a world long after these two events took

86

place and with which they have had no personal experience.

The same is also true of the three or four major religious denominations, depending on how you count them, which arose in response to specific American conditions at the beginning of this century and have become trapped by the taint of denominationalism which separates rather than unites. The youngest and most recent denomination on the Jewish scene which owes its birth to the teachings of Mordecai Kaplan is now headed by a newer generation who are scholars of hasidism, mysticism and committed to a far greater role of spirituality in religious life than Kaplan would have countenanced. The Conservative Movement is engaged in a demoralizing battle between those who view themselves as essentially *not* Orthodox and those who view themselves as predominantly *not* Reform. It is entirely conceivable that given a different set of dominant personalities, the Conservative Movement in the United States might have become like the United Synagogue in England with a more liberal tinge. If Reform Judaism in the early part of the century had preserved a greater attachment to Jewish peoplehood and the tradition, a large part of the present Conservative Movement might have identified itself with them.

I could cite variations of this scenario, namely, that the present constituencies within our religious movements are chafing at the bit with what they consider their confinement to an ideology which does not necessarily reflect their current yearnings and aspirations.

The same can be said of most of the community relations agencies such as the American Jewish Committee, the American Jewish Congress and the Anti-Defamation League, most of whom are in the process of redefining their agendas and priorities. Space does not permit me to analyze the changing functions and agendas of the Federations.

The fact is, however, that two processes have been at work within the American Jewish community in recent decades with an accelerating pace: (1) decharismatization and (2) decentralization. An observer of the American Jewish scene would note that all of the living leaders with charismatic personalities and authorities are aging octogenarians and older, like Salo Baron, Moshe Feinstein, Louis Finkelstein, and Joseph Soloveichik. I suspect that the same is true in Israel and elsewhere. Does this mean that there aren't people alive today who are as learned, as pious and as competent as the aforementioned, or does it mean that our community refuses to bestow this kind of authority on new individuals who may have all the requisite talents and attributes?

We have become a community which is suspicious of authority figures, a relic of the sixties with creeping anti-clericalism and the growing assertion by the laity that they know as much as or more than the professionals whom they engaged to administer their various institutions in their communities. There is very little doubt in my mind that the role of the American rabbi is in the process of undergoing a considerable change from that of a communal leader, authoritative spokesman, to a more limited role as pastor, synagogue administrator, ritual authority and religious role model. It is too early to tell whether this may be good for religious life or a setback.

The same is true for the roles of the various community relations agencies, which, in the past, at least, claimed a monopoly on access to government and other non-Jewish authorities. Today, almost any community in the continental United States has one or more Jewish businessmen or professionals who have easy access to the White House or their local Senators and no longer need to turn to special intermediaries like Jacob Schiff, Jacob Blaustein, or Stephen Wise to perform this service.

I recently heard from an historian who was going through the Eisenhower papers that the only Jewish leader with whom Eisenhower met at all during his eight years as President was Abba Hillel Silver. Ronald Reagan has been confronted with a wider variety of Jews in public and in private than all of his Republican predecessors combined.

Accompanying this process of decharismatization has been an accelerated process of decentralization of the central religious institutions, theological seminaries and rabbinical organizations. Congregational structures have become increasingly weakened while their local congregations have become stronger and less dependent on their central institutions for guidance and leadership. The same process is happening in other communal and Federation agencies. As each Federation becomes more involved in community planning and funding of community programs, including those of Jewish content, they turn less and less to their national headquarters.

To cite a few examples: the growing number of Federations, beginning with San Francisco and Los Angeles who have opened up their own offices in Jerusalem, thereby by-passing their dependence on national agencies like UJA or UIA. It is fair to predict that this process will continue with each community concentrating more on direct relationships with sister institutions in Israel, Washington, and other centers and not necessarily use their national organizational channels. Another example is the growing number of Jewish communities who are appointing learned Jews like Rabbi Richard Israel to enhance local Jewish resources for the Jewish community centers in Boston, which makes it less necessary for local Jewish community centers to depend on JWB for guidance on Jewish programs.

Paradoxically, with the blurring of denominational lines in America, on the one hand, and the growing militant separatism, on the other, Israel emerges as a more viable and accessible symbol and reality of Jewish unity. The educational institutions in Israel, especially those which are not tainted by denominationalism, can become increasingly vibrant resources for Jewish spirituality, education, and values. Another paradox is that Israel can become the center for unifying Jewish values, while the Diaspora, especially in the United States, must assume a greater burden for *aliyah*.

Let me elaborate and cite some examples. If a new prayer book is published in America from anyone like Artscroll to the Rabbinical Assembly, it immediately takes on a denominational hue and becomes inaccessible to those of opposing denominations. On the other hand, if an Israeli academic institution of higher learning produces a curriculum for the teaching of Siddur (Prayer book), it can be used by the Reform in Australia, Hasidim in Sunderland, and Conservative communities in Iowa. After all, we all recite the same Sh'ma and the basic structure of the Siddur is a shared heritage, not a divisive one. Each denomination can continue to publish its own Siddurim to reflect their own ideologies, while the inherent values of the Siddur can be extrapolated and disseminated from Israel. At the same time, the problem and the challenge of increasing *aliyah* from North America must be handled by the communities of America. It is interesting to note that more and more Federations are establishing loan funds and other programs for direct assistance to the present and future *olim* in their communities.

Goldscheider correctly points to the declining religiosity and traditional religious practice among the younger generations. I am not sure about religiosity if by that is meant the quest for the spiritual and the yearning for the transcendental. It is true that many traditional Jewish practices are being more zealously observed by a hardcore minority of Fundamentalist Jews and ignored by a growing number of others. It is also true, as Goldscheider points out, that other selected rituals have emerged which command wide observance.

The time may be right to sponsor a new kind of Jewish population study that will deal not only with Jewish demographics but also to ascertain an emerging pattern of widely observed *mitzvot* which may be different than the priorities given to other *mitzvot* by earlier Jewish generations. It would be fascinating, for example, for an in-depth study of Jewish leaders, geographically and chronologically diverse, to see what are the Jewish *mitzvot* to which they give absolute obedience and to which they attach lesser importance. A new Shulchan Aruch (religious guidebook) might emerge reflecting a considerable consensus about the priorities and Jewish obligations which a constituency of philanthropists share.

I believe that such a study would also find that what is emerging is a greater desire for intimate spiritual community as opposed to the impersonality of the rootless, with mobile populations who are born in one community, educated in another, and settle in a third. This is true from the extreme right to the far left from what some Orthodox observers call *shtiebilization* to the growth of the chavura movement in the non-Fundamentalist religious camp.

There is no doubt that the past decade has witnessed a widespread *baal t'shuva* movement which cuts across all denominational lines. Only the Fundamentalists have been prepared with a ready set of rituals and curriculum for those willing to drop anchor in their midst. The broader Jewish community has not yet provided adequate funding, facilities, and programs for the tens of thousands of questing Jews who are not willing to cut themselves off from the rest of the world but want to remain in a world that welcomes pluralism and yet provides sanctuary to those seeking community, intimacy, sharing and caring.

There is no doubt that the great tasks which the decades ahead will demand of us require the quantity and quality of personnel which our community has not yet developed. Such people exist. Ways must be found for seeking them out, nurturing them, enlisting their support for what I believe is just the beginning of another golden age of the Jewish spirit.

DEBORAH DASH MOORE
Vassar College

Goldscheider rightly identifies the components of the assimilation perspective, its implications; and its link with one of the most influential and successful Jewish ideologies of modern times. When he turns to the alternative view, which probably deserves a name, he is equally acute in presenting its components but disavows an ideological commitment. Here I disagree. I think that there is an ideological commitment grounding what I will call the continuity thesis. Furthermore, this ideology is very close to the Zionist posture of those who see a dying American Jewry; in fact, it is a variation of Zionism. It is the ideology of those spiritual Zionists who can trace their intellectual lineage through Israel Friedlander to Ahad Ha'am and Simon Dubnov on the Jewish side and to such pluralist thinkers as John Dewey on the American side. While the continuity theory, or the idea of America as the new diaspora center, is not necessarily an outgrowth of cultural Zionist ideology, the theory's interpretation of facts certainly reflects this ideological perspective. At least one could say that the two are congenial. Back at the beginning of the century Friedlander compared American Jewry to a sick person. The Zionists prescribed moving to a new more healthy climate; the assimilationists planned for the funeral. But American Jewry was too sick to move and too well to commit suicide. Friedlander, and his associates, proposed a third alternative, one which in many ways resembles Goldscheider's perspective.

Now there are, of course, differences, and I would not want to minimize these. Most importantly, Goldscheider points out that social scientists recognize now that modernization creates new bases of ethnic and religious cohesion in pluralist societies. I do think, however, that it would be useful to retain the concept of collective assimilation, especially when talking about how assimilation has led to stronger ethnic group cohesion. This would allow us to distinguish the trajectory and consequences of individual assimilation--both for the individual and the group--from the path and result of collective assimilation. Same word, different processes.

I wholeheartedly second the advocacy of a comparative perspective. It is crucial. A variety of comparisons also encourages new insight and challenges standard patterns of thinking.

I question the assertion that there is a direct correlation between interaction in larger numbers of spheres of activity and greater ethnic group cohesion. As is done further on in the essay, this type of statement must be qualified. There are other variables needed to allow interaction to encourage cohesion rather than conflict or disaffection.

I find the discussion of the structural basis for Jewish distinctiveness to be excellent. I think it would be useful to link this analysis with a discussion of how American Jews interpret Jewish distinctiveness. I have in mind both Mirsky's suggestive essay on American Jews' view of themselves as a chosen people with its disturbing effect on the provision of Jewish social services to the deviant (a chosen people has no pathologies) and Eisen's thoughtful account of rabbinic efforts to reconcile chosenness with the perceived demands of a democratic society. Such issues are germane, as well, to the debate over Jewish day school education (even the avoidance of the term "parochial school" merits comment). In short, there is an ideological and theological aspect to Jewish distinctiveness that should be noted.

I have little to add to the fine analysis of Jewish marginals. I would note that not only is there no "deep-rooted ideological base favoring out-marriage," but that the reverse is often true: intermarried Jews who identify as Jews often prefer their children to marry Jews. They do not see their intermarriage as a model for their offspring. I would also underscore the remarks that intermarriage is not "particularly selective of the less committed" and that differences between intermarried and non-intermarried

94

"have *narrowed* over time."

I am curious why residential dispersal and integration no longer weaken informal ties to the Jewish community. How do we explain this shift? Is it due to the distinctions that are made between formal and informal community? I would add an historiographical note that the focus on the benefits of residential segregation reflects a revision of previous attitudes emphasizing the cost of such segregation. What we need is what is advocated--a balanced view, not another swing of the pendulum. Similarly, I would point out that Jews do differ from non-Jews in their response to housing markets, life cycle demands and economic constraints, though Goldscheider is right that these general factors are clearly associated with Jewish residential distribution. And Jews do attribute values to their residential distinctiveness (as they do to their socioeconomic and political distinctiveness), although these values do not dictate their migration patterns.

While I agree that the definition of Jewishness according to biology or Halacha is becoming less important for American Jews, it remains important for Israeli Jews. Hence, the controversy over "who is a Jew" will probably not disappear for a while. This should be kept in mind.

I do not understand why defining cohesion as interaction should lead to policies that might result in the vacuity of Jewish organizational activities.

An historical point: first generation east European Jewish immigrants to the United States did have large families, larger than the normal for white Americans. The second generation reduced family size drastically.

I have many nods of agreement with the important points on Jewish socioeconomic distinctiveness vis-a-vis non-Jews, on the importance of the job for Jews, on generational similarity, on Jewish women's distinctiveness and on the impact of college education on Jews.

Here I will pause and try to tie together my responses to the comments on the last two items. Jewish women, visible finally after many years, are pursuing careers, raising families (albeit at later ages) and living longer lives. These three aspects must be

95

considered together. Jewish women's organizations need to respond to the new demands of professional working women as well as to the needs of active senior women. In both cases it is relevant to consider the possibilities for Jewish cultural activity--adult education classes, lectures and forums, and other cultural expressions. I think of my aunt, childless, areligious, in her late sixties, who devotes hours each week to Hadassah and finds Jewish meaning in this traditional voluntary activity. I also think of my grandmother, in her late eighties, religious, who pursues courses on all sorts of subjects (including crafts, birdwatching, literature, Hebrew language) not under Jewish auspices. She endows her activity with Jewish meaning--e.g., crafting silver candlesticks, spice boxes, menorahs. There are obviously many other variations but proposals for institutional changes must take into account the scope of Jewish women's activities, from young adulthood to old age. Similarly, the relationship of American and Israeli Jewish women can include interaction between American Jewish and Israeli feminists, professionals and volunteers. This will not be a symmetrical relationship, but I do not think that Israel-American Jewish relationships can be symmetrical. There are both pragmatic and ideological problems with the concept of symmetry. I hasten to add that dependency is not the only other alternative. I would urge that shared time--residency for Israelis in the United States and for American Jews in Israel--be encouraged and promoted for men and women of all ages. This would increase the fluency of more American Jews in Hebrew--vital if anything approaching symmetry is to be achieved--and would create new contexts for understanding emigration/immigration. It might also encourage attitudes endorsing the complementary aspects of American Jewish and Israeli societies.

I strongly endorse the proposal for modern Jewish studies, especially at those American colleges that attract the future Jewish elite. Jewish studies can be encouraged by American Jewish organizational contributions, as well as individual efforts; in fact these are probably critical to the success of instituting or expanding Jewish studies on American campuses. Modern Jewish studies is a vital tool to reach marginal Jews as well, and I would expand that category to include the non-married and widowed. Adult Jewish education under university auspices should also be promoted. There is an appalling dearth of positions in American Jewish history (my own field)--I believe that only the rabbinical seminaries have full-time appointments in this field--which reflects in part the bias of academic Jewish studies toward the classical and medieval periods. Jewish students, at least the one's who attend Vassar College, are particularly drawn to the study of contemporary Jewry for reasons connected mostly to their own identity formation, yet most existing Jewish studies programs fail to recognize the importance of such study.

I am perplexed why so little space was devoted to a discussion of religious activities. These need to be strengthened and enriched. Innovation ought to be encouraged. American Jewry lacks the constraints of a religious establishment and lies in an environment conducive to religious experimentation, and is thus uniquely situated to develop new modes of Jewish religious expression. The institution of Bat Mitzvah is a case in point. There are other possibilities: e.g., new ways of celebrating Sukkot to restore that holiday to a place of importance on the American Jewish calendar. Another example: the summer program in Israel which is proposed and which I like (it reminds me of the successful two-week program in Israel for marginal Jewish academics that has had a significant impact on both the individuals involved and their campuses) might have a biblical orientation rather than an eclectic one.

Of the three specific policy proposals, I think that it is easiest to implement the modern Jewish studies one because the colleges and universities are receptive to Jewish studies (that battle was fought in the '70s) and there is an academic organization headed by Moshe Davis that is able to assist on intellectual and substantive matters. The summer program for teenagers seems to me to be the most difficult to implement because of the challenge of defining who is marginal to the Jewish community and because of the ambivalence among American Jews about focusing their monies and energies on such risky individuals. I find it difficult to assess the leadership proposal. My impression is that a number of these problems are recognized by American Jewish and Israeli leaders and that some effort is being made to implement programs with components similar to those contained in this proposal. Perhaps we can assume that leaders will think about themselves and their problems, and turn our energies instead to those who are scarcely aware that they represent problems for American Jewry.

97

BERNARD REISMAN
Brandeis University

Statistics can have a strong deterministic influence on people's attitudes and behaviors. A typical example was evidenced in the meeting of the European Council of Jewish Communal Services I attended in May 1985 in Florence, Italy. The Council is an umbrella organization of the Jewish communities in Great Britain and Europe with the goal of sustaining these Jewish communities. The keynote speaker, who opened the Council's annual meeting, was a demographer from Israel. He presented data from research currently being conducted at the Hebrew University, which points to a steady decline in Jewish population in every country where Jews now live, except for Israel.[1] The combination of low birth rates, intermarriage, and assimilation are inevitably leading to an erosion of the population of each Diaspora country as well as a decline in the total Jewish population.

As might be expected, these data had a very depressing impact on the European communal leaders at the meeting. They are already well aware of the many problems which confront them in trying to sustain their Jewish communities. But when, in addition, they are confronted with information which says that they are part of an enterprise which is inevitably doomed, it is, to say the least, difficult to mobilize one's energies. One could sense among the European leaders a sense of resignation and despair.

Subsequent events at the meeting added another interesting dimension to the leaders' responses. Following the session on demography was a panel presentation in which representatives from six European countries reported on new programs and evidence of resurgent Jewish interest in their countries. However, in the wake of the earlier grim demographic forecast, the "good news" didn't make much of an impact. I spoke the next day. As my point of departure I picked up on a caution noted by the demographer as he concluded his analysis. He said: "We can't really predict the future; we can only extrapolate from recent trends. Further, you should know there are important variables which are subject to reversal. If people change their attitudes there can be changes in the current trend."

My message essentially was that it was up to the leaders to decide how they wanted to deal with the demographic data. They could accept them as inevitable, in which case they would become a self-fulfilling prophecy. Or, if they felt it important to sustain their Jewish communities and were prepared to work to try to change those uncertain variables, maybe they could "avert the severe decree." Their response was enthusiastic, which I quickly add was not because of the eloquence of my speech, but rather because my message reached the instincts of the leaders for the survival of their communities. I brought words of hope, the prospect of being able to control one's destiny.

It is important to analyze the psychology of the responses to these demographic projections. There is more here than straightforward, objective facts and rational responses. In the first instance there is an aura of unimpeachable expertise which accompanies the prescription of the demographers. Despite their own caveats, sometimes noted in very small print, their words take on a tone of gospel (or should I say Torah) truth. In part, this response may be explained by the complicated and esoteric ways contemporary demographers gather their information and come to their conclusions. It is understandable that the layman would be cowed and deferential. Further legitimacy is added to the results of the demographer's work by the enthusiastic response they elicit from the Jewish media and from rabbis and other "official" Jewish voices. Dire projections make for wonderful sermons and news stories. Some Jewish organizational leaders have become dependent on such periodic messages of gloom as a way of upgrading the flagging interests of their members.

A case in point was the response to the article which appeared in *Midstream* in 1977 and which predicted, based on the work of Harvard demographers, an American Jewish community in 2076 that "is likely to number not more than 944,000 persons, and conceivably as few as 10,420."[2] There was a media and platform blitz in the American Jewish community featuring these doomsday projections. Despite the fact that the demographic procedures utilized in this piece of work were thoroughly discredited by other demographers, for many years after, up to the present, one still encounters these statistical "facts."

The connection between what people are led to believe is possible by "experts" and how they will subsequently behave is obvious. The instincts of the European Jewish leaders, and I might add, my own, were that not only did they want a more favorable future prospect for their Jewish communities, but they had some emerging evidence which suggested it might be achievable. So, when another expert legitimated their survival instincts they were invigorated and ready to get on with their work.

Problem: suppose the Israeli demographers are correct; suppose the decline in Jewish population they project is indeed inevitable, regardless of the attitudes and energy mobilized by the Jewish communal leaders. In that case, is not optimism giving false reassurance and likely to lead to policies which would be misguided and futile?

Now comes the demographic analyses of Calvin Goldscheider and Steven M. Cohen.[3] Without repeating the themes of Goldscheider's work, represented in the essay and monograph upon which it is based, suffice to say that he looks at current demographic data for the American Jewish community and comes up with different projections, ones which suggest that the future population of the American Jewish community will not decline and may even increase. One could argue that Goldscheider is wrong, and that is possible, but so too is it possible now to argue that the alternative demographic projections are wrong. Or, one could argue that America is different and that Goldscheider's projections would not apply to other Diaspora communities. Perhaps not; but even if the pessimistic demographic projection for America were proven faulty, that in itself would be significant, given the important role of the American Jewish community in contemporary Jewish life.

101

Goldscheider's case rests on new data as well as different techniques for reading and interpreting data about the critical variables which lead to assimilation--low birth rate, intermarriage, and the status of Jews who live in areas of low Jewish population density. These variables are critical in determining the rate of assimilation of Jews in any culture. While Goldscheider doesn't project his findings outside of America it is at least reasonable to assume they may have relevance to Europe, Latin America, or other free Diaspora communities.

In any event the work of Goldscheider and his colleagues suggests that the pessimistic demographic forecasts, at best, represent one school of thought and could be either overstated or wrong. As a result, for me, and I suspect other Jewish leaders, the authoritative expertise of the pessimistic demographers has been demystified and their heretofore exclusive hold on defining Jewish population has been dislodged. Perhaps this development will be translated into a freeing up of Jewish energies for creative future social planning. Indeed, Goldscheider has also provided a number of specific demographic findings which call for new policy and programmatic approaches. In this concluding section I address policy and programmatic implications for the American Jewish community emerging from Goldscheider's data.

Policy and Program Implications

1. *New Demographic Studies*

Given the importance of demography in shaping attitudes and policies in the Jewish community it is vital that community leaders have available to them accurate data. Much of the data with which Jewish demographers now work are either dated (the National Jewish Population Study was conducted over 15 years ago) or based on secondary analysis of fragmentary Jewish samples from general American population studies. Recently positive initiatives have been taken by the Center for Modern Jewish Studies at Brandeis University and the Council of Jewish Federations to coordinate the several local American Jewish community population studies.[4] It would be very helpful to launch a new national Jewish population study which could provide accurate information for assessing trends in Jewish life and for planning. Also, such a major study might test out different approaches and theses of the two (or more) demographic schools of thought.

2. *Family*

Goldscheider's data affirm "that the family remains a powerful basis of community among Jews and continues to be one of the major sources of group continuity." While the primacy remains, it is a different family, with new needs to meet if it is to fulfill its expectations. Five areas of family programming are suggested for attention by Jewish communal agencies: (a) *Matchmaking:* Designing services which are appropriately sophisticated to help interested Jewish young adults in finding appropriate mates; (b) *Two-Professional Marriages:* Providing support to what is emerging as the most typical marital pattern for Jews now marrying - the two-professional couple; (c) *Day Care:* Making available quality day care under Jewish auspices to meet the needs of single or two working Jewish parents and to provide positive Jewish learning in the child's critical early years; (d) *Surrogate Extended Families:* Supporting havurot and similar intentionally created surrogate extended families which can be helpful to the growing numbers of family units without access to their own extended homes; (e) *Divorce:* Strengthening community services to minimize the adverse effects of divorce, a growing problem in the Jewish community. Such services should seek to: enhance communication among couples, help resolve conflicts, and encourage divorcing couples to approach the process in ways which are not disabling to them and their children.

3. *Synagogues and Jewish Schools*

Goldscheider makes the observation that the synagogue and the Jewish school, in addition to their traditional functions of transmitting Jewish content and serving as a place to observe Jewish rituals, also are "contexts for Jewish interaction." In these settings Jews not only learn about their heritage but they also establish social ties with other Jews and build a cohesive community. It is therefore desirable that leaders of synagogues and Jewish schools are helped to create settings which foster and nourish social relations, and this objective is appreciated as an important institutional role in assuring Jewish continuity.

4. *Jewish Marginals*

One of those demographic variables which is amenable to change depending on community policies are the "Jewish

103

marginals." The terms refers to those Jews who are not in the mainstream of Jewish life, and, depending on how they are approached, can either remain marginal or can be more closely integrated into the community. The major group of Jewish marginals are the intermarried. Their integration would be helped by efforts to encourage the non-Jewish individual to convert or by efforts to help the Jewish community be more accepting of intermarried families--converted or otherwise. Another group of Jewish marginals which Goldscheider indicates would be receptive to community outreach are Jews living in areas of low Jewish density.

5. *The University*

A basic theme Goldscheider stresses as important for Jewish continuity is the opportunity for Jews to interact with other Jews, to be part of a Jewish community. He reminds us of the extraordinarily high proportion of American Jews who attend university (90 percent). This is a time in the life cycle when critical choices are being made about one's life pattern--vocation, mate selection and core values. Further, typically in America young people attend universities away from their home communities. Many also will attend graduate school so the period of time at the university can range from four to eight years. Without some Jewish connection during these years, the university experience can become a passage out of Jewish life for the potential leaders of the next generation.

These facts point up the importance of upgrading the priority the American Jewish community attaches to providing quality services for Jewish university students. The issue needs a national perspective so as to even out the financial burdens of serving students by those communities which have large concentrations of Jewish students attending universities in their area. The growing presence of courses in Jewish studies at universities is a valuable resource in influencing favorably the Jewish identity of students and merits financial support from the Jewish community.

6. *Israelis in the U.S.*

There is a "non-issue" in the American Jewish Community which needs to be addressed openly--Israelis who have chosen to live in the United States (Yordim). Many of these Israelis live in a state of Jewish limbo, on the margins, lacking official status in either the American Jewish community or Israel. Marginal Jews need both interaction with other Jews and the awareness that they are wanted if they are not to drift out of the Jewish community. Given that the number of such Israelis living in America is large (estimates range from 100,000 to 300,000), the Jewish people cannot afford the erosion of this important population group. American Jewish leaders, in collaboration with the appropriate Israeli officials, should begin the process of reaching out and establishing links with Israelis living in their communities.

7. *Israel and the American Jewish Community: Symmetry*

Several policy considerations emerge from the demographic analysis about relations between Israel and the American Jewish community. Basic to formulating these policies is the need for a clarification of the nature of the relationship between the two communities. The key word is symmetry. Israel and the American Jewish community are the two vital sources of Jewish energy and influence in the world today. It is important that both communities view each other as partners, understanding their differences, their respective strengths and weaknesses, and how they can interact with mutual respect for their individual benefit and for the benefit of the Jewish people.

Israel has been a major source of shaping the Jewish identity of contemporary American Jews. The American Jewish community should continue to expand its visits and programs of study in Israel, for all age groups, as a way of strengthening their Jewish identity. At the same time, Israel should explore ways in which it can use the American Jewish community as a resource for its own educational agenda and particularly for strengthening ties between Israeli and American Jews. Goldscheider points out that in the past generation there have been growing demographic divergencies between Israeli and American Jews. Efforts need to be directed to fostering greater interaction so as to sustain the sense of community between Jews of the two countries.

As in any relationship it is well periodically to review the changes which have occurred with both parties over the years and to modify the terms of the interaction. Both Israel and the American Jewish community have changed over the past 37 years and it is time to review those changes and to assure that the

105

relationship progresses to an appropriately mature level. For American Jews, change will call for their taking themselves and their community more seriously and responding to their Israeli brethren as peers rather than as reverential junior partners. For Israelis, change will call for their acting on their verbal commitments to a symmetrical partnership, for demonstrating in behavior a respect for the American Jewish community and for pursuing ways they can learn from their American Jewish brethren.

8. *Ideology*

Goldscheider comes to a conclusion from the data with which I do not agree. He moves from evidence of "declining religiosity and ritual practice among the younger generations" to conclude: "There seems to be little doubt about the growing secularization of American Jews." Accordingly his prognosis for the future bases for Jewish continuity leans heavily on ethnicity and Jewish communal ties in America and with Israel. My contacts with younger generations of American Jews suggest that there is a great interest in Jewish religious/spiritual links, although not necessarily in the same way Jewish religiosity and spirituality have been expressed by prior generations. Young people are forming their own Jewish networks--havurot, minyanim--to seek out Jewish religious definitions which are both authentically Jewish and consonant with their modern, intellectual values. These young people seem to be much less secular than their parent's generation. They appear to recognize that for Jews ethnicity may not be enough to sustain the community. They are seeking to define and make accessible the transcendent dimension of Jewishness. This ideological quest within the Jewish tradition warrants the encouragement and support of the organized community, particularly as there may be a waning of the eternal sources of Jewish identity, which have been so important in defining the Jewish identity of recent generations of American Jews: the Holocaust, Israel, and anti-semitism.

106

REFERENCES

1. U.O. Schmelz and Sergio Della Pergola, "World Jewish Population, 1982," AMERICAN JEWISH YEARBOOK, 1985.

2. Elihu Bergman, "The American Jewish Population Erosion," 5MIDSTREAM, October 1977, p. 9.

3. Steven M. Cohen and Calvin Goldscheider, "Jews, More or Less," MOMENT, September, 1984.

4. Gary A. Tobin and Alvin Chenkin, "Recent Jewish Communal Population Studies: A Roundup," AMERICAN JEWISH YEARBOOK, 1985.

JONATHAN D. SARNA
Hebrew Union College

Professor Goldscheider's thought provoking paper continues the pathbreaking re-evaluation of American Jewish life he set forth in several earlier books and articles. His thesis and the data undergirding it have begun to be seriously discussed in academic circles, and it seems likely that this discussion will be further stimulated by the recent publication of Charles Silberman's long-awaited *A Certain People,* that comes to somewhat similar conclusions. A new and far more positive view of American Jewish life is crystallizing.

To be sure, there are dark clouds on the American and Jewish horizons that cannot be ignored. I particularly miss any discussion here of the growing trend toward polarization of the American Jewish community, particularly along religious lines. One may disagree with the evidence put forward by Reuven P. Bulka in *The Coming Cataclysm* (1984) and underscored by Irving Greenberg in his "Will There be One Jewish People by the Year 2000" (1985). To ignore their warning altogether, however, seems to me to be foolhardy. My own view is therefore somewhat more centrist than Goldscheider's. I see many of the positive developments in the American Jewish community that he does; indeed, I believe that we are in the midst of what may properly be called a "Great American Jewish Awakening." On the other hand, I see negative aspects of American Jewish life as well. Without pretending to know what the future holds, I agree with Goldscheider that it is neither predetermined nor certain. It depends upon policies now being formulated.

Before discussing the specific proposals that Goldscheider puts forward, I should like briefly to discuss two points that I think help to put his analysis into perspective. First of all, we must remember that all analyses of the future carry with them a certain element of self-negation. Predictions are no sooner uttered than community leaders react to them. For this reason, what Professor Goldscheider calls "the Assimilation Perspective" has actually functioned as a decidedly positive force in American Jewish life. Precisely because so many researchers have gloomily predicted American Jewry's coming disappearance, more money than ever before has been pumped into areas like Jewish education and culture. The turnabout in American Jewish life that Goldscheider and others now notice stems at least in part from actions undertaken in response to past alarms. Without implying that social scientists should shape their predictions on the basis of potential community responses to them, one must nevertheless realize that too sanguine a view of American Jewish life today could set the stage for a reversal of current trends. If American Jews become so smug that they refuse to provide further support for the institutions that have brought about the community's welcome renewal, the current awakening may prove tragically short-lived.

Second, the welcome trends that Professor Goldscheider notices are in some part due to a great ideological change occurring in the general American community. Nagging evidence of persistent anti-Semitism notwithstanding, recent decades have seen a spectacular rise in what might properly be called the "new philo-Semitism." One of the reasons for the rise in intermarriages is thus that some non-Jews now *seek* to marry Jews--that is one way of gaining entry into a community that boasts a high status in contemporary America. From the point of view of cultural and intellectual life, to be a non-Jew is seen by some actually to be a disadvantage since it deprives one of important kin connections. According to James Atlas, writing in the New York Times Magazine (August 25, 1985), "Kentucky-born Elizabeth Hardwick has often claimed that she came to New York in order to be a Jewish intellectual, and (William) Barrett describes in "The Truants" an atmosphere so 'pervasively Jewish' that he tended to forget he was 'not a Jew after all.'" The subject requires a deeper analysis than can be undertaken here; still, it is important to recognize that this atmosphere of philo-Semitism need not be an everlasting one. Should the status of Jews in America decline, it is reasonable to assume that some of the trends Goldscheider notices, particularly those related to intermarriage and Jewish identity, could swing back into earlier assimilationist patterns. Ours, after all, is not the first Jewish revival in American Jewish history. Past experience suggests that positive trends give way sooner or later to negative trends--what evangelist Charles Finney called "backsliding." Leaders of the Jewish community must be prepared for this eventuality.

Let me now turn to Professor Goldscheider's three policy suggestions: 1) He suggests first and foremost a "summer program for unaffiliated teenagers." The idea of reaching out to marginal Jews is, of course, a laudatory one. I fear, however, that any proposal that devotes a disproportionate percentage of Jewish communal resources upon one group--and especially a group marginal to the community--has no hope whatsoever of winning approval. Furthermore, since resources are limited, I must assume that this program would take money away from other much needed resources--probably educational and cultural institutions. My own suggestion, therefore, is that each Jewish community set up a fund to support a *full range* of educational and cultural programs geared to Jewish teenagers. Some might dip into this fund for programs of the kind Goldscheider suggests. Others could use it to support Jewish day school expenses. Still others might call on it to fund a Jewish summer camp experience in the United States, or some other potentially valuable program yet to be devised. By making available a large endowment of this kind from which various kinds of activities for Jewish teenagers could be funded, a Jewish community would be making a critical statement about its priorities. At the same time, it would be encouraging a full range of options aimed at enhancing the Jewish life of all those in this critical age group, while allowing individuals to avail themselves of whatever options seem best suited to their personal needs and goals.

2) Goldscheider's second proposal, to devote increased funds to support Jewish studies programs in colleges and universities, will find far greater appeal. Hundreds of these programs in fact already exist, and new ones are being funded all the time. Considerable prestige attaches to a donor who gives money to a non-Jewish university for support of Jewish studies; as a result, this kind of program proves particularly attractive. From the point of view of philanthropy, Jewish studies programs may be seen as the "Jewish hospitals" of the 1980s. The future of these programs, at least in the short run, seems certain.

111

There is an important secondary function of Jewish studies programs that deserves mention. Almost all of these programs should have added to them (as most do) some adult Jewish education component. Whether the Jewish studies program organizes a lecture series, an adult education course, or a full non-credit program for adults, there is in each case a recognition that Jewish studies departments have a communal responsibility quite apart from their responsibility just to college-age students. Given an increasing desire on the part of universities to improve "town-gown" relations, and a growing sophistication of the American Jewish lay public--most of which, as Goldscheider indicates, is college-trained--there need be no lessening of standards in community outreach programs of this sort. To the contrary, adult Jewish education can be raised up to a new level of excellence. An added benefit of this proposal might be the reintegration of Jewish academicians into Jewish policymaking bodies. It has by now been widely recognized that the separation of academia from the policymaking centers of Jewish life has worked to the detriment of both. By supporting Jewish studies programs aimed at least in part at bringing community figures into contact with Jewish scholars, reconciliation might begin to be effected.

3) Goldscheider's final proposal, to implement programs designed to overcome the increasing chasm between American and Israeli leaders, is unlikely to find many detractors. Reading between the lines, however, it is clear that Israelis know far less about their American counterparts than the Americans know about Israel. I fully agree with Goldscheider that "a greater (Israeli) appreciation of the rich Jewishness of American Jewish life, the cultural and social cohesion of the community, the diversity of religiosity and ethnic expression would go far in bridging a widening gap." To my mind, however, that end would better be served by the creation in Israel of a well-funded "Center for the Study of American Jewish Life." It would be the function of such a center (1) to disseminate material on American Jewish life to those in leadership capacities, (2) to make certain that Israeli educational textbooks contain adequate and reliable information on American Jewish life, and (3) to foster research and discussion on issues of concern to the two communities. Leadership development along the lines that Professor Goldscheider suggests could certainly be included among the functions of this center, but much more than that is needed.

My disagreements with some aspects of Professor Goldscheider's paper notwithstanding, I want to conclude by commending him for his bold effort to redirect American Jewish communal policy along new and I believe more effective lines. Professor Goldscheider realizes, as most others in the American Jewish community do not, that the "survivalist agenda," with its narrow focus on issues like anti-Semitism, assimilation, and intermarriage, has outlived its usefulness; from the perspective of the 1980s it is far too narrow. Goldscheider's new and more positive perspective on American Jewish life, coupled with his innovative policy suggestions, should result in a new agenda for the American Jewish community. Instead of worrying about whether there will be an American Jewish community in the year 2000, we can now move on to the far more significant question of what *kind* of Jewish community it will be--and what steps we can take to improve its quality. Redirecting community thinking and resources along these lines--without becoming self-satisfied or reckless and while remaining on guard against negative communal developments--will help ensure that the American Jewish community of tomorrow remains strong, culturally vibrant, and intellectually creative.

ALEXANDER M. SCHINDLER
Union of American Hebrew Congregations

Professor Goldscheider's evaluative study of the "health" of the American Jewish community today is a welcome addition to a field dominated by pessimism. His paper, with its positive emphases, should serve as a valuable tool for self-reflection and encouragement among Jewish communal and religious leaders, particularly as a response to the work of Israeli scholars whose perceptions of American Jewry remain biased by their adherence to the classical Zionist approach, which holds the disintegration of Diaspora communities as inevitable. His study also corrects the pessimistic views of an earlier school of American Jewish sociologists who but a decade ago predicted our community's imminent disintegration.

Unfortunately, I have not been able to examine the two studies undergirding Dr. Goldscheider's conclusions. I cannot, therefore, comment on the accuracy of all of his material. I am, rather, at the mercy of an essay without footnotes. Nonetheless, my own perceptions and intuitions, refined as they are by extensive work in the American Jewish community, confirm Dr. Goldscheider's central thesis: Our community is alive and well. It obviously has its aches and pains, but these are growing pains, not symptoms of impending demise.

My own quibble with Professor Goldscheider pertains neither to his facts nor his interpretations, but with his somewhat defensive characterization of his study as "not the rejection of one ideological position, replacing it with another...not simply a question of the glass being half-full or half-empty...not an interpretation of optimism versus pessimism..." Methinks the scholar protests too much, and unnecessarily. Evaluations of the status of Jewish identification must involve subjective judgments as is clear in the ongoing struggles over Israel's Law of Return and the sectarian exclusion of Reform and Conservative Judaism from the mainstream of Israeli life. What is "health" to one set of Jews is "decadence" to another; what is "extremism" to one group is halacha to another. I am therefore skeptical of Dr. Goldscheider's intention to have his conclusions read as scientific; moreover, I do not want to be deterred by such intentions from putting some of his optimism to the test.

First, however, let me amplify it.

Numerically, the American Jewish community has not declined. In fact, it appears we are growing in strength. Two decades ago we saw a spate of articles foretelling otherwise. Both *Look* and *Life* magazines featured pieces that spoke of the "Vanishing American Jew" and warned that by the year 2000 we would be less than half a million strong. Well, we are nearing that millennium and we are ten times that number. It is *Look* magazine, not its Jewish readership, that has vanished, while *Life* survives in but a truncated form.

Three reasons were advanced for our impending demise: the rapid rise in the rate of intermarriage; a disturbing decline in our birthrate; and the attenuation of our identity. In other words: We intermarry too much, we have too few kids, and with each generation we become less involved in Jewish life. Happily, these forebodings proved incorrect. More recent research on all of these crucial issues allows us to be far more hopeful.

The rate of intermarriage has not increased as dramatically as we once feared. Those doomsday figures which were thrown about but a decade ago (an intermarriage rate of 33 percent, of 50 percent, of 70 percent) have now been corrected to the 25-30 percent level. The figure is still great and grave but the increase is, at least, now in arithmetic rather than geometric proportions. Moreover, the rate of conversions to Judaism has tripled over the past five or six years, and an ever-increasing proportion of the children of intermarriages are being reared as Jews. Included among our conversions, by the way, is a steady increase in people who choose Judaism on religious grounds alone, not because they

116

are married or about to be married to Jews, but because in their quest for meaning they have discovered and eventually embraced our faith.

An increasing number of Jewish sociologists are thus convinced that intermarriage is no longer a drain on our numeric strength--quite the contrary, that it has actually become a means of our enlargement. As Dr. Steven Cohen recently put it: "Don't forget, mathematically speaking, intermarriage could conceivably *double* the number of Jews." Such remarks clearly demonstrate that we've come a long way from the brink of extinction.

The much-bemoaned declining birthrate among Jews has also proved to be chimerical. For the past decade or so we were told that the Jewish birthrate is 1.7 children per couple--below the national average and certainly below the replacement level. These projections, however, were based on comparisons between young, Jewish married women in the 1950s and their equivalents in the 1970s. This failed to account for the fact that Jewish women today are having their children later in life. Those who appeared as childless or one-child couples in the 1970s have by and large become as fertile as the Jewish couples of an earlier generation. It appears, therefore, that the birthrate is simply not a significant issue.

The attenuation of Jewish consciousness therefore becomes the only critical threat to the American Jewish community--if, indeed, it exists as a factor or trend. In general, I am pleased with Dr. Goldscheider's conclusion that it does not: that the prediction of a "gradual and continuous erosion of Jewish cohesion" in America is simply "inconsistent with empirical evidence." I appreciate the broadmindedness with which he views "family ties, economic networks, social bonds, educational background and residential patterns linked to lifestyle, interaction and ethnic community" as positive evidence of persistent and even resurgent Jewish self-awareness. In his urge not to be taken for a subjectivist, however, Dr. Goldscheider passes up several opportunities to polish his argument.

For example, I miss in his discussion mention of the American Jewish community as a political community--that is, as a predominantly liberal, politically active, socially conscious group. Certainly on the question of political support for Israel our community views itself as an activist group. Thus, for instance, you will often find an Alex Schindler of the Reform movement and a Moshe Sherer of the Aguda joining hands on the same side of the table. But more than support for Israel or for the struggles of Soviet Jewry is involved in Jewish political identity. There is no doubt in my mind that Jews are aware of their disproportionate involvement in social and electoral movements. We joke about it, take pride in it, bemoan it, relate to one another through it. Political apathy, that weakening virus of democracy, is anathema to American Jews; we are immune to it. Thus we are linked to each other in our reading habits, our ethical discussions around the dinner table, our concern with anti-Semitism and racism, our wrestling with issues of conscience.

Liberalism has been the glue of that self-awareness for decades. Even our neoconservative figures were launched into their careers from the pad of liberalism--a fact that tends to make their conservatism less predictable, more multi-faceted and morally compelling than traditional American conservatism. In a sense, Jewish liberals and Jewish conservatives listen with the same ear and consider as central the same issues. This is a thread of Jewish identity that Dr. Goldscheider ignores, despite overwhelming evidence, such as the fact that Jerry Falwell managed, with just a few comments about "Christianizing America," to alienate nearly 25 percent of the Jewish vote that might otherwise have gone to Reagan in 1984.

Similarly, Dr. Goldscheider makes entirely too short a shrift of philanthropy as a centripetal force for our community. The *pushka* of old has been replaced by 501(c) (3) of the Internal Revenue Code, but *tsedakkah,* tax-exempt or not, remains a given in Jewish life. It is not merely wealth, but generosity--a tradition of responsibility and obligation--that makes the Jewish community so valuable a funding source for causes both mainstream and Jewish. That generosity is part of the soul of American Jewish identity.

Even while Dr. Goldscheider omits mention of these positive sources of Jewish identification, he overemphasizes others, with little substantiation. There is a certain glibness to his emphasis on "interaction" as the underpinning of Jewish identification; he defines the Jewish content of such interaction very shallowly, and without much historical context. For example: a how-d'ye-do at the work place between fellow Jews might indeed be a daily reminder of Jewish identity for those workers. Compared, however, to the work place bonding among Jews two or three generations ago--when the Yiddish language, the concentration of Jews into certain industries, the commonly suffered exploitation, the struggles for labor unions, etc., created an entire Jewish milieu--a brief conversation at the water cooler today is certainly a tenuous bond. What, truly, is the stuff of modern, job-related Jewish identity? I get more optimism than definition from Dr. Goldscheider on this one.

Similarly, one could argue (Dr. Goldscheider does not) that the penetration of Jewish artists into the mainstream culture has helped bring marginal Jews into contact with "Jewish things." Woody Allen, Saul Bellow, Mel Brooks, Philip Roth--these and other artists reveal and utilize their Jewish identities in their work far more openly than the Jack Bennys of the past. In general, one could say, the mass media is a cohesive force for American Jewry. But one would have to evaluate that claim as positive or pitiful based upon historical comparisons (to the hey-day of Yiddish theater, for example) as well as an analysis of the *content* of modern "Jewish" art. If its effect is to replace assimilationism with Jewish self-deprecation--well, that is a form of Jewish identity, but it makes our task of community building no easier.

For guidance in defining policy, in other words, I feel that I need a deeper evaluation of the content of Jewish interaction than Dr. Goldscheider's paper gives.

His "Policy Perspectives" section is nonetheless helpful as a general orientation, as it emphasizes the quest for continuity and creatively and uses Israel-Diaspora relations as a positive force for Jewish identity-building. I would, however, redistribute some of his programmatic emphasis. Outstandingly, I regret that Dr. Goldscheider has chosen to deal only superficially with the question of mixed marriages. While I am pleased with his conclusion that intermarriage should be viewed as "more of a challenge and less as a threat to Jewish continuity," I fear being complacent about the issue. Challenge must be met or it transforms into danger rapidly. Moreover, challenge must be met *before* panic sets in, so that our creativity, intact, can serve us. In this spirit, Reform Judaism's Outreach program was established seven years ago. Its effectiveness has contributed to those demographic benefits (increased conversion and so on) to which I alluded earlier. Such a program should serve as an inspiration and foundation for greater Jewish outreach efforts, for the inundation of mixed marriages in the American Jewish community will undoubtedly be a significant factor in the shaping of our future and our identity in the 21st century.

Dr. Goldscheider's emphasis on marriage and the family as fundamental to the demographic survival of American Jews is significant, but here, too, his programmatic approach appears to me to be too narrow. He enjoins that the Jewish community efforts focus on college youth, on the role of women, and a bit on the children of the intermarried. But what about singles, and single-parent families, which have mushroomed in the past three decades? Their relative need for attention is infinitely greater and should receive a higher place on the community's scale of priorities for research allocation.

Indeed, Dr. Goldscheider's recommendation for the strongest possible enrichment of Jewish Studies programs on American campuses, while in and of itself commendable, is disproportionate. There has, after all, been a veritable explosion of such studies since World War II, thanks to those munificent resources provided by the American Jewish community to universities through the length and breadth of the U.S. Unhappily, these investments have not been as fruitful to the community as we might have hoped, possibly because those who occupy the various chairs of Judaic Studies have been more faithful to academia's canons of objectivity than they have been heedful of the needs of the Jewish community. In my judgment, therefore, there is a greater need for redirection than for expansion in the field of Jewish higher education.

Let us move beyond these programmatic particulars, however, to discuss the underpinnings, the motivations, the spiritual content of our outreach work. What feeling or sensibility need we project as a Jewish community both to marginal Jews and our own dissatisfied members? I'm afraid that Dr. Goldscheider exalts "interaction" between Jews as the *summum bonum*. But that approach to the health of our community is simply too narrow and non-holistic. What is the source of that interacting? How long will it last? Is such interaction, devoid of its ideological-religious rootage, really worth the struggle and sacrifice and martyrdom ofttimes required for Jewish survival?

Dr. Goldscheider's upbeat message does not recognize the pain and alienation that American Jews, like many Americans, suffer today. It does not recognize the quest for meaning that has become the guiding spirit of the age. It does not acknowledge the religious impulse among the highly educated stratum of young American professional Jews, as well as an ever greater manifestation of their yearning for more traditional modes of Jewish expression. This is what will give Jewish interaction its power and future: our communal offer of relief from alienation, our spiritual bonding, our balanced and holy calendar, our religious values.

The religious dimension must play a far more powerful role in Jewish continuity than Dr. Goldscheider would have us believe or would, presumably, acknowledge. The temper of our times is infinitely more congenial to religious spirit. Christian thinkers and contemporary philosophers have called for the reintroduction of ethical values in society based on the recognition of some transcendent reality. Even progressive secular thinkers are eagerly seeking the roots of their world views. Creative interpretation of religious texts and teachings is cresting. Indeed, the schism between fundamentalists and liberal religionists in general has become as key on the world historical stage as the religious-secular schism of the past three centuries.

There simply is no denying it, then: the synagogues of our communities, be they Orthodox, Conservative, or Reform, along with their schools, should be assigned the highest possible priority on the scale of American Jewish philanthropic endeavor. For who is responsible for teaching our children to be Jewish? Who will assure that there will be a Jewishly educated, Jewishly committed generation two decades hence? Who will provide the teachers and rabbis and scholars for that generation? Who will provide the impulse for those networks of Jewish interaction of which Dr. Goldscheider speaks? Who will provide the State of Israel with a continuing corps of understanding Jews? The answer, in every case, is the synagogue. It has to be the synagogue--the synagogue and those camps, seminaries and multitudinous educational endeavors which they sustain.

Just as we begin our cycle of Torah reading anew in the autumn of each year, we face anew the task of Jewish continuity and regeneration in each generation. Analyses such as Dr. Goldscheider's should help us to recognize--and a crucial recognition it is--that we are not at the end of something, but at the beginning of our next stage as a community. Perhaps the book of *Genesis* can be our guide in this recognition, as it returns us to the individual men and women, the individual consciences, the individual experiences of God, that began the line of Jewish continuity under the rainbow of the Covenant. Perhaps, before we can move ahead, we must return.

CHARLES E. SILBERMAN,
Author

The most important, and in some ways most controversial, argument in Professor Goldscheider's paper may well be its premise: that the formulation of Jewish communal policy "requires fundamental knowledge" about the social, economic, demographic, cultural, and religious trends within the community. The premise ought to be self-evident--so much so that one would hardly think it needs to be stated. Yet the reality is that although the gap has begun to be remedied in recent years, the Jewish community has conducted remarkably little research about itself, and--more serious--has tended to ignore the evidence that is available. All too often, research results are cited (it would be too much to say "used") only when they seem to bolster existing prejudices and preconceptions; data that run counter to these preconceptions are simply ignored.

Consider, for example, the current discussion of population growth and decline. There is hardly a communal leader who does not "know" that we are in the midst of a catastrophic population decline; as evidence, those who discuss the issue continue to cite the now-famous 1977 *Midstream* article by Elihu Bergman indicating that by 2076, the Jewish population of the United States would be no higher than 944,000 and might be as low as 10,420. (I have been present at discussions at which only the lower figure was used). In his own jeremiad on the subject, also published in *Midstream,* Professor Robert Gordis has written that he is "unaware of any convincing refutation of (Bergman's) procedures or...conclusions," ignoring the fact that one of the

123

demographers responsible for the projections Bergman used refuted both the procedures and the conclusions in the pages of *Midstream* itself! But Gordis, who is certain that the "situation is... desperate," believed that "precise figures are not the issue," since "the trend is indisputable." But precise figures are precisely the issue, since without them we cannot know the trend, which, as Goldscheider demonstrates, is quite different from what Gordis and most others assume.

I cite this not to criticize Robert Gordis but to suggest the magnitude of the gap between policy-makers and scholars.[1] This gap, in turn, points to the one weakness I find in Goldscheider's paper: his underestimation of the magnitude of the ideological and psychological problems inherent in persuading communal leaders to base their policies on the knowledge that scholarship can and does engender. "The argument is not simply a question of semantics," Goldscheider writes. "...It is not the rejection of one ideological position, replacing it with another ideology. It is not simply a question of the glass being half-full or half-empty. It is not an interpretation of optimism versus pessimism. It is an interpretation of new social scientific evidence about ethnic cohesion, which has led to a revision of older theories...

Would that it were so! My own experience suggests that ideology and pessimism play a larger role than Goldscheider suggests, albeit an unconscious one. One of the crucial insights of perception psychology, after all, is that perception is more than just an objective phenomenon, i.e., more than a relationship between the individual and the object in sight; we see what we are prepared to see--what our experience or our preconceptions enables us to see. "The nervous system is not the one-way street we thought it was--carrying messages from the environment to the brain, there to be organized into representations of the world," Jerome Bruner has written. "Rather, the brain has a program that is its own...specifying different priorities for different kinds of environmental messages. Selectivity is the rule and a nervous system...is as much an editorial hierarchy as it is a system for carrying signals."

----

[1] Gordis is a scholar, of course, but in a different field.

124

The "editorial hierarchy" of the American Jewish communal "nervous system" makes it difficult for leaders (and in my own experience, even harder for members of the rank and file) to see the evidence that Goldscheider and others present. Specifically, their pessimistic mind-set blinds all too many American Jews to the evidence, and thus to the policy alternatives that flow from it. Much as I would like to believe that the problem is simply one of looking at, and interpreting the evidence--for I myself find the evidence overwhelmingly persuasive--I fear that the problem is far more difficult. If policy-making is to be improved, we will have to do more than present the evidence and indicate the policy alternatives that arise; we will have to change the mind-set that enables Jews to see and hear only the bad news and that leads them to ignore (and at times, it would seem, to want to silence, if not necessarily to slay) the messenger who brings them good news.

That being said, let me emphasize that I agree with most of Goldscheider's policy recommendations. His comments about intermarriage, for example, are critically important, for they reflect research data demonstrating that intermarriage now occurs in a radically different environment than in the past--so much so that past experience provides a poor, perhaps even misleading, guide to the present. The fact that intermarriage no longer is associated with disaffection from Judaism means that the consequences of intermarriage for Jewish continuity are not pre-ordained. How Jews respond--individually and collectively--can help determine whether intermarriage contributes to, or harms, Jewish survival. Hence the critical importance of Goldscheider's argument that "intermarriage needs to be understood less as a threat to Jewish continuity and more as a challenge for Jewish communal policies."

I also wish to second Goldscheider's argument that Israeli policies toward American Jewry must "reflect the fact that the American Jewish community is a powerful source of vitality." I would add a second argument: That although American Jews have much to learn from Israel, the reverse is equally true--and badly neglected. One need in no sense argue that specifically American approaches and institutional arrangements be transplanted to Israel to suggest that Israeli Jews can learn invaluable lessons--in the present climate, in fact, critically important lessons--by giving careful study to the nature of Jewish religious pluralism in the United States. It is equally important for Israelis in general to make the startling discovery that the young Israeli leaders who have visited the United States in recent years under the auspices of the American Jewish Committee have made: namely, that contrary to the Israeli stereotype, American Reform and Conservative and Reconstructionist Jews are often far more religiously observant than most Israelis, as well as deeply committed to the concepts of Klal Yisrael and Netzakh Yisrael.

One last word: although there is a long and honorable tradition of pessimism in Jewish life, as Simon Rawidowicz pointed out in his essay on "The Ever-Dying People", it is worth noting that although only a small minority of the 12 spies brought back an optimistic report, and although the Israelites as a whole wanted to stone Joshua and Caleb to death, it was the optimistic view that prevailed. Indeed, the majority of pessimistic spies died of the plague, as God's punishment for their pessimistic reports on the future of the Jewish people.

IRA SILVERMAN
Reconstructionist Rabbinical College

While I do not agree at all with the various doomsday prophesies about the "vanishing American Jew," I cannot, on the other hand, endorse the rather rosy analysis and prognosis offered by Calvin Goldscheider in his paper on "The American Jewish Community: Social Science Research and Policy Implications." My less optimistic view calls into question some of the implications of that paper, although its policy recommendations need not be seriously altered as a result.

"The American Jewish community is a forceful and cohesive community," write Goldscheider; so far, so good. "It has strong anchors of social, religious, and family life; it is neither vanishing demographically nor weakening Jewishly." It is this latter point that I believe the array of survey data will not support.

Most powerful in undermining that thesis are the findings of Steven M. Cohen presented in *American Modernity and Jewish Identity* (Tavistock, 1983). They show a continuous decline in measures of Jewish identity and participation over time and across succeeding generations of American Jews. Despite some stabilization for the "fourth generation," that decline is not really arrested. The most hopeful finding of Cohen's research, I believe, is that new forms of Jewish expression are being developed, to replace evidently unattractive traditional forms--a sign of Judaism's continued evolution in America. These new expressions, new modes of observance and identification, are, in my opinion, exciting but quite fragile. Nonetheless, they may

127

indeed serve to yield the kind of Jewish cohesion, distinctiveness and vitality which Goldscheider foresees.

Nathan Glazer, writing recently in *Commentary* (August 1985), shares a more pessimistic outlook "even if by some measures--Jewish day schools, programs of Jewish studies, Hanukah candles--the level of identity and cohesion seems high, the main tendency is in the other direction...We have been told that Judaism in America is in a line of historic continuity and represents no decisive break with the past, that it is different but still the same. In my judgment this argument is too optimistic. Less and less of the life of American Jews is derived from Jewish history, experience, culture, and religion. More and more of it is derived from the current and existing realities of American culture, American politics, and the general American religion."

This may not be bad--in fact, from my own Reconstructionist perspective it may in some respects be desirable--but it is not, I am afraid, solid ground for the kind of forecast underlying Goldscheider's analysis. Without going into specific detail, given the requested emphasis on the policy issues, I would question what I believe to be overly optimistic inferences regarding: the Jewish attachments of the intermarried; that of other marginals; the relative unimportance of geographic community; and Jewish divorce trends.

It is not clear, however, that my less sanguine view would call into question the thoughtful and creative policy suggestions offered by Goldscheider. In fact, a marginally more pessimistic analysis would probably simply increase the need for and the urgency of such well-tailored programmatic proposals to increase Jewish identification, affiliation, etc.

In that vein, I fully concur with the stated policy objectives, i.e., that they should enhance the cohesion of the Jewish community, enhance general continuity, and enhance the multiple forms of relationships to Israel.

Where I begin to diverge is in the definition of target populations. While I fully appreciate and support the objective of reaching out to the marginals, my own preference is to focus on strengthening the depth and richness of Jewish commitment of Jews closer to the committed core.

Without wishing to trivialize the matter, I have thought of American Jewry as resembling a jelly doughnut: flaky and crumbling around the edges, but sweet and sticky in the center. I suggest there is not really much we (organized Jewish agencies) can do about the flakes, but there is much we can do to augment the center. It can be argued, to prolong the metaphor, that those in the core are already stuck and will continue to adhere, willy-nilly--but much needs to be done, in reality, to keep people there and to transmit that adherence from generation to generation.

I am therefore less interested in focusing so heavily on the marginals, assuming limited resources for the projected programmatic activities. I nonetheless agree with the choice of program avenues, i.e., family life and Jewish education. (I am less clear about what can be effectively done in the third stated avenue, demography, although one can hardly gainsay the desirability of better outreach to Jewish college students, the Jewish aged, the newly arrived Jewish immigrants.)

Nor would I cast doubt on the value of the three specific policy recommendations offered; a summer program for unaffiliated youngsters; support for modern Jewish studies in universities; and the development of new relationships among the Jewish leadership in Israel and the United States. They all seem to me to be selfevidently worthwhile. Having said that, I would offer the following additional thoughts about them.

A. With respect to the summer program for teenagers, I would repeat that I would focus less on the really marginal types that seem to be suggested, and more on children of families with more highly developed Jewish sensibilities--even if the children themselves are not affiliated with such "Jewish youth groups" as USY, NFTY, Young Judea, BBYO, etc. (A personal note: I was such a teenager--unaffiliated but from an affirmatively identifying Jewish family--who was "turned on" by a summer program, in Israel, organized for unaffiliated teens).

I would also demur on the suggestion that such a summer program be free of charge. Quite apart from the heavy communal burden implied by that proposal, I firmly believe that programs are taken more seriously--and are viewed as much more desirable--when they are offered for a fee, and possibly for an expensive one, at that. "Scholarships" could of course be available, but participants with financial capacity should pay.

129

The suggested focus on Israel and Zionism should certainly be part of such a program, but we need to keep in mind, I believe, the need to create and sustain an American approach to Judaism which can stand not wholly on its own--Israel will always be viewed as our people's ancient and modern homeland--but without depending on vicarious Israeli nationalism to provide a virtual surrogate religion. Thus a broader focus on our people's full history, our shared civilization, and its religious expression, seems to be in order.

B. As for modern Jewish studies in American universities, the general validity of the proposal is selfevident. Nonetheless, I should want to keep in mind, lest expectations be overly inflated, the warnings issued by several American Jewish scholars, including most notably, Jacob Neusner. If the notion of the American university as a secular, dispassionate setting for rational inquiry is to be sustained, then the study of Judaism and Jewish civilization there, while in itself fully appropriate, cannot be expected to engender personal commitments of faith and identification on the part of students. The study of Judaism may inspire interest on the part of some, but it will not--should not--entail a conversion experience.

Advocates of such a goal would, in Neusner's words, misunderstand "the character of university education in the West, where the university teacher's goal is not to indoctrinate but to educate. Education does not gain preset goals, let alone conclusions reached in advance of analysis and argument. It does not serve principally to persuade students about their personal lives and commitments. It is not meant to serve political or religious causes, however praiseworthy. It is not an instrumentality for a purpose set outside of the campus of the university. ("Misunderstanding or Contempt?", *The Jewish Spectator*, Spring 1985).

Like Neusner, I do not know how, through Judaic studies, to reconcile the divergent goals of the university and advocates of enhanced Jewish identity and commitment. Augmented university studies in Judaism should be supported, but our communal expectations about their achievements in terms of the Jewish identity formation of the students must be appropriate and limited.

C. The suggested approaches toward enhancing the relationships between American Jewish and Israeli Jewish leadership seem to be on target. They do not, however, go far enough toward prescribing actual policies and programs. My own predelections are for *vastly* enhanced programs of (physical) interchange, including summers and full years of visits by American Jews to Israel *and by Israeli Jews to the U.S.* I emphasize the latter because policies to date have been directed only at bringing American to Israel, and, for (I suppose) obvious reasons, never the reverse. If we are to educate our communities *mutually* about each other, then the exchanges should be mutual. Israeli Jews can usefully learn much about American Jews, about Judaism, even about Israel from extended experiences in the U.S. The reverse is well known.

To support such a program of mutual exchange, entailing groups at all age levels, would require a reallocation of communal resources, but would be worth it. At a minimum, much of the funds sunk unproductively into encouraging an altogether unlikely North American *aliya* should be re-directed into facilitating these more limited exchanges which may result, in time, in a sort of "quasi-aliyah" of backing and forthing. This may come to characterize the relationship between interested American and Israeli Jewish leaders, and may be a highly desirably mode of Jewish connection.

Beyond this proposal for rather massive action, I would augment Goldscheider's only by. concentrating, as suggested above, the proposed educational programs in the U.S. on an already somewhat interested population. The best outreach models we have may be those, like the Judaic programs of New York's 92nd Street Y, which start by enhancing the richness of Jewish experience for Jews already interested in their Jewishness--and then become so appreciated and magnetic that they, by status and word of mouth, attract countless others. There are already such "pockets of Jewish energy" in (a few) synagogues, havurot, centers, and so forth. Those successful models should (simply?) be identified, studied, and replicated whenever and wherever possible. I would suggest such a study/program project as being a useful component of subsequent program planning.

JACOB B. UKELES
Consultant on Jewish Affairs

Professor Goldscheider's basic thesis is sound: the doomsday scenario with regard to the future of the Jewish community in North America is wrong. All of the available evidence from research and policy practice supports his view that the Jewish community is not likely to disappear nor to weaken drastically as an American subculture. Jewish institutions are likely to be reasonably vigorous, and Jewish identity is not likely to melt away in the American crucible. Even a casual reader of Jewish history is aware that the threat of catastrophe is always present; our community is not immune, but hopefully catastrophe is improbable.

I have two difficulties with Professor Goldscheider's presentation.

In his zeal to counteract the prophets of doom, he understates current problems. For example, he underestimates the threat of intermarriage to the cohesion of the Jewish community; he too glibly dismisses the concern about the size of the total Jewish population; and he overstates the importance of interaction among Jews as *the* measure of community.

His analytic framework for social policy development does not relate to the decision-making system within the Jewish community nor to the agenda as seen by those in that system. This point will only become clear with illustrations, which will be developed below.

My agreement with the basic thesis should not be obscured by these areas of disagreement; I concentrate on the latter because a recitation of areas of agreement would be less likely to stimulate further discussions.

Current Problems

A. The Threat of a Divided Community

Professor Goldscheider presents the new tendency among sociologists and demographers studying the Jewish community to minimize the negative impact of intermarriage. This tendency is based on some evidence that intermarriage *per se* may not cause Jews to be "lost"; the relatively lower rates of intermarriage in some of the largest metropolitan areas such as New York; and a reinterpretation of some of the data used by alarmists to show a disappearing community.

This approach misses the point about intermarriage: intermarriage is not a problem because of "losses" but because different attitudes toward intermarriage and conversion exacerbate the divisions within the Jewish community, in an environment where intermarriage has become commonplace. It is difficult to believe that intermarriage is not increasing; certainly all of the anecdotal evidence seems to suggest that there is more intermarriage in the Jewish community in the United States than twenty years ago. This means more non-Jewish spouses and children of mixed marriages. Is a non-Jewish spouse or child of a mixed marriage to be accepted in the community? Is a commitment to convert to Judaism required for acceptance? What definitions of Jewishness and ground rules for conversion apply: halachic or non-halachic ones? There is a potential for schism around these issues probably not seen in Jewish history since the Karaite movement. There is real risk that the statement, "the Jewish Community" will lose meaning with this loss of cohesion as large numbers of self-defined Jews are not defined as Jews by others.

B. The Size of the Jewish Community in North America

Debunking the "disappearing Jewish community" myth, does not fully put to bed the issue of the size of the Jewish community from a policy perspective. It is impossible to make a policy judgment without a value judgment about how big the community ought to be. It is also a mistake to confuse the issue of whether we *can* do anything about the size of the community with the issue of whether we *should*. If the community is large enough, then trying to enlarge it is irrelevant; if the population is seen as much too small, then perhaps we have no alternative but to try to increase it. In any event, it seems to me that it is a mistake to take the aggregate size of the community off the policy agenda at least until there has been a thorough debate about what constitutes an optimum size Jewish community in North America.

Assuming a Jewish community of between four and one-half and six million, if current trends continue, at least three different values are relevant: from the point of view of critical mass for identity and continuity it is probably big enough; from the point of view of Holocaust losses, it is tragically small; and from the point of view of political clout, continuing growth is necessary. Could we affect these numbers if we tried? We don't know because we haven't tried. If the Zero-Population Growth movement was able to discourage people from having children, it is not clear that a concerted pro-natalist movement could not encourage people to have children. Such a pro-natalist movement might have an impact on the marginal decision-making of Jewish households deciding between two and three children.

C. Interaction, Identity and Community

Professor Goldscheider places great stress on the "interactive" measure of community; and separates religious and ethnic measures of Jewishness. Both of these judgments are questionable. A more useful view is that interaction with other Jews is only one form of affiliation and that religious observance and affiliation are different dimensions of Jewish commitment and by extension, Jewish identity. Most Jews appear neither strongly committed nor uncommitted, they appear to be somewhat committed, that is they are "the marginally affiliated." Measures of commitment (both observance and affiliation) seem to increase with family formation and child rearing; the supposed secularization of American Jewry does not hold up when identity patterns are analyzed by age and family status. While interaction among Jews (e.g., friendship patterns) is high, there is no evidence that it is any more important in shaping the Jewish community

135

than other forms of affiliation (e.g., reading Anglo-Jewish newspapers, contributing to the UJA or visiting Israel).

The Linkage between Social Science and Policy

The most serious problem with the Goldscheider paper is the underlying policy research model. It presumes that one collects information, analyses it, draws policy-relevant conclusions, develops goals and designs policy. He postulates goals: whose goals are they and what entity are they supposed to guide? He discusses choosing target populations, but it is unclear by whom and where in the policy-making process are target groups chosen? The choices he poses, such as the choice between "core" or those at the margins, do not seem to be implicit or explicit choices actually faced in Jewish communal policy-making. The program recommendations such as a liaison organization to college youth seem unconnected to what is going on such as the increasing regionalization of Hillel and the greater involvement of local communities in their college campuses. In short, the policy analytic model presented seems poorly suited to real-world policy-making.

A better policy analytic model starts with a review of the policy-making environment: who is making the policy and for whom; what types of resources are available to implement policy; who are the key actors and what are their interests. Policy is not created in a vacuum. The second step in community policy analysis is to define the policy agenda: what questions or issues are on the table, i.e., what are the important choices that the organization or system is confronting, and what conflicts about appropriate future directions have emerged from the tussles of constituencies over priorities? Having defined an agenda of policy questions in a particular policy-making environment, then research can begin: information about important aspects of the community and its needs can be collected and analyzed and brought to bear on the agenda and the environment. Policy options are formulated which might resolve issues, probable consequences assessed, criteria of choice explicated, and the pros and cons of recommended policies presented.

The Jewish policy-making process is highly fragmented. Except for the international agenda it is also highly localized as well. In each local community, there are multiple centers of

136

decision-making centering on, but not limited to, the local Federation and its affiliated agencies. While there are national agencies in particular subject areas (such as NJCRAC for community relations), they tend to be coordinative and advisory rather than agencies which can make and implement national policy. The subject area focus is also limiting; many issues either fall between the cracks or involve duplicative and uncoordinated efforts. Perhaps the American Jewish community needs a domestic analogue to the Conference of Presidents which at least has the potential of some modest comprehensive policy-making or strategic planning. Given the localized nature of the current system, the policy-making process and policy agenda in every community is different.

The most one can say about this policy agenda is that there are overlapping and, in some cases, common themes. The program of the General Assembly of the Council of Jewish Federations is probably the best summary of these common themes running through the current Jewish policy agendas in various communities. The most recent General Assembly, held in Washington, D.C. with over 3,000 participants, covered over 75 separate topics ranging from (A)dolescents to (Z)ero-population growth. Some of the policy issues on the table in this system which seem to be of strategic importance include: Jewish poverty and near-poverty, which is hidden but substantial; quality community care for the aged and disabled in an era when families are dispersed and therefore not available for decisions or care; the development of new alternatives to the traditional supplementary school and strategies for identity-building for marginally-affiliated adults; strategies of minimizing the disruptive impact of intermarriage on community cohesion; and programs of support for family cohesion and growth.

On an organizational level, Jewish communities need to think through issues of roles and resources: how to cope with the declining role of the Federal government in human services; how to set priorities in the face of relatively weak campaigns--how to allocate resources between Israel and local needs and how to balance investments in human services versus community-building; how to respond to the geography of Jewish life--via decentralization and neighborhood preservation; how to balance the "Jewish" agenda with the increasing need to work with other ethnic groups and public agencies to provide human services.

137

A framework for Jewish policy planning can be built in every Jewish community around these issues of content and process. Such a framework needs to accommodate strategic planning for the future along with short-term reaction to specific pressures and problems.

Professor Goldscheider's paper is less a policy agenda or tool for providing policy and program direction than a collection of enormously enriching insights into Jewish communities of North America. His contribution should be appreciated by researchers as well as by those involved in the policy arena.

PART THREE

EPILOGUE

Calvin Goldscheider

RESEARCH AND POLICY FOR AMERICAN JEWS: CLARIFICATION AND RESPONSE

Objectives

My objective in preparing the original essay, "The American Jewish Community: Social Science Research and Policy Implications," was to try to generate policies and programs from the emerging evidence on the sociology of American Jews and their communities. In the process, I wanted to link specific policy recommendations to a new understanding of the contemporary American Jewish community and demonstrate that social scientific research has profound implications for the ways in which patterns of social change in the Jewish community are invoked and interpreted in policy formation. My goal was to be suggestive and provocative; to show how the accepted interpretations of American Jewish life informs our orientations to policies and programs. In particular, I wanted to suggest that a different view of the processes of social change and continuity among American Jews would have different policy implications.

I reviewed the patterns of American Jewish life that were emerging without detailed empirical documentation in that essay. Some of the findings remain controversial and await retesting and evaluation by scholars studying the American Jewish community. I have documented the evidence and data elsewhere and these can be evaluated on their merits. My goal was not to describe and evaluate existing policies or policy-making institutions and programs in the American Jewish community. It is clearly of

141

great importance to know who sets the policy goals, who they guide, who chooses the targets for policy implementation, what resources are being invested and whose interests are being served. While the analysis of those issues would be a valuable exercise, it would require a different focus and systematic new research, as well as competence of a different kind. I wanted to suggest different ways of looking at the Jews of America and at the communities they have formed, provide a new interpretation of what I found emerging out of the detailed statistics, and propose a reappraisal of the evidence. Primarily, I wanted to bridge the gap between social science research on American Jews and policies and programming directed to enhancing the quality of American Jewish life.

We asked researchers, historians, sociologists, religious and secular leaders, and policy makers to respond to, and comment on, the analysis and particularly the policy implications. I am pleased that they found the materials interesting and provocative and that they responded with care and thoughtfulness. Some built on the analysis by providing new arguments and alternative policy suggestions. These policies and programs, along with those made in the original essay, should be thoroughly evaluated.

There are major areas of overall agreement among those who commented on the original essay. Yet all of those who responded and reacted disagreed with one part or another of my analysis or with some of the policy suggestions. But the disagreements were not uniform: where some saw weak arguments, others found agreement. Where some were encouraging of a particular suggestion, others found the policy ambiguous, limited, or simply wrong. From some perspectives, my analysis went too far, or was misleading; others found that the analysis did not go far enough and was "defensive". What some defined as issues characterizing marginal Jewish segments, others defined as issues of the core within the American Jewish community. The heterogeneity among responses reflects part of the variation within the American Jewish community and the wide range of opinions, perspectives, and orientations of those who were responding. The disagreement among the responders and between them and the ideas, suggestions and analysis contained in the original essay is to be encouraged. It is a sign of great health, indeed of communal vigor, that the issues can be debated, that differences can be aired, and alternatives can be posited.

142

Some of the disagreements among the responses reflect differences of perspectives or priorities. In some cases, the issues of disagreement are related to differences of strategies, rather than goals. Often there is not a clear sense of what might work best in the context of the complex and variegated American Jewish organizational structures. We remain far from achieving a consensus about policy goals and we know little about the efficiencies of policy implementation within the voluntary institutional structure of the American Jewish community. Nor do we have evaluation research to test models of program impact and long-term effects of policies. Until more is done along the lines of evaluation and assessment, we shall have to tolerate a wide range of policy ambiguities.

I do not agree with all the critical remarks, and I want to take the opportunity in this epilogue to respond to selective points raised by others. It is obvious from some of the comments that parts of the materials in the original essay were not as clear as I wanted them to be. I want to clarify these and focus more sharply on areas of agreement and disagreement. I hope that this type of dialogue continues in a variety of forums and expands among these observers of the American Jewish community and among others.

Caveats and Biases

An overall caveat should have been included in the original essay which should have been stated clearly and unambiguously: Many of the patterns of American Jewish social life which I described (and in the detailed statistical documentation upon which the essay was based and which was published elsewhere) are limited by the data available. All empirical evidence has limitations in design, scope, depth, method, measurement, and coverage. The sociological study of the Jews is no exception to the general qualifications of social science research. Some of the patterns described are based on evidence from individual, often "unrepresentative", communities. Some of these patterns may not characterize the American Jewish community as a whole. In part, an examination of national patterns averages differences among communities and neutralizes some of the rich and important variation at the local level. Often we do not know how biased these community studies are since comparative studies are lacking. Other patterns, derived from national data sources, lack depth and include only a small number of Jewish respondents. Some findings are based on controversial data, from biased samples, using less than adequate methodologies. Often these are the only data available to examine a particular pattern. Other conclusions have been inferred from threads and strands of evidence, and thus in a formal sense should be viewed as hypotheses rather than as rigorously tested conclusions. I have often asserted the emergence of a particular pattern or trend without the necessary qualifications and cautions appropriate for scientific exchanges. Nevertheless, I am convinced that the whole picture I describe is an accurate account of emerging patterns of fourth and fifth generation Jews in the 1980s and that these patterns are empirically documented in recent research. These patterns are new and demand revisions in the overall interpretations of American Jewish life. Nevertheless, it is clear that we continue to need research on critical parts of the emerging patterns. In particular, we need better evidence on generational and life cycle patterns. Systematic data are required to help assess the future implications of marriage and intermarriage and the social, family, economic, and cultural networks which link Jews to their communities. We need as well systematic data on the generational transmission of Jewish values. These data will require an entirely different methodological approach and research design than the simple cross-sectional orientation so common in Jewish community studies.

My goal was not only to review what we know but to link what we know, however imperfect and limited, to policies directed to change and intervention, to enhance and improve the cohesiveness of the Jewish community, and increase the quality of Jewish life so as to ensure not only the survival of the community but its creative development. Policies in the Jewish community have often been designed in a social science vacuum or more seriously have been based on a misunderstanding of social scientific evidence. Existing policies have been organized around an implicit conception of the future of American Jewry and implicit "theories" of what factors determine the cohesion and continuity of the Jewish community. Hence, even without solid scientific data that would satisfy rigorous methodological criteria, policies are taking shape and programs are being implemented. In that context, my objective was to reorient our planning and our thinking about the future based on a solid foundation of an assessment of our past, to describe and interpret what social scientists know, even as we recognize the limitations of that

144

knowledge.

The only ideological commitments reflected in the analysis are those associated with the canons of social science. My interpretations of the data are based on my reading of the evidence and couched within the framework of social science theories. To be sure, these theories and orientations are biased in the sense that the social sciences are based on a set of assumptions about how to study communities. But as in all scientific research, we present our methods and research design, describe and analyze our data, and draw our conclusions. The extent to which our findings can be tested, replicated, incorporated within conceptual frameworks, determines how close we approximate the model of scientific inquiry. There may be ideological and broader theoretical frameworks that can be attached to the emerging perspective that I have presented. That is a less serious critical point than the suggestion made by some that I am ideologically biased or motivated by ideological commitments. I argued that there was a consistency between the assimilation perspective and the Zionist ideology, or at last one dominant variant of Zionism. I have no doubt that there were and are ideologists who have formulated interpretations of Jewish life similar to that which I have presented and ground them in a systematic ideological framework. Ideology, however, does not guide my analysis. If others are committed to a particular ideology, let that commitment be explicit. If ideological orientations guide our policies and our priorities, so be it. But then we need to argue out the relative merits of ideologies to determine the relative priorities of programs and policies. In any case, let us not couch our ideological commitments in the guise of social science or in the framework of dealing with an assessment of the realities of American Jewish life.

Clarifications: Social Science and Policy

What are the major issues that require clarification? The most severe challenge posed in these responses (and by others who read or heard in lecture form various parts of the original essay) was to my fundamental assessment of the American Jewish community. I tended to pose the question at the extremes: Is the American Jewish community "robust"? Or is the American Jewish community dying? Most agree that the Jewish community in the United States is not moving toward total assimilation and is therefore not dying, but there is some disagreement about whether I exaggerated the strength or robustness of the community. Similarly, others have raised the question about the weakening quality of Jewish life and the generational decline in knowledge of Judaism and Jewishness. I argued for a definition of Jewish cohesion based on the extent and depth of ties and linkages among Jews. The greater the extent of ties, in the larger number of areas of social life, the stronger and more cohesive is the community. But some disagree with those criteria and have raised the question of the depth and permanence of bonds that are not primarily anchored in religion or in cultural consensus and tradition. What are American Jews willing to sacrifice for economic, social, and family ties? Can the bonds of lifestyle and casual interactions sustain the next generation? In the crudest sense, can interaction of Jews in the swimming pools of Jewish community centers be treated as a basis for Jewish communal cohesion if there is no Jewish cultural content? Haven't I committed the error of painting too rosy a picture of the American Jewish community? Am I not being overly optimistic in ways that mirror the errors that I claim have been made by those who have been overly pessimistic?

Perhaps an analogy will help clarify my argument. In World War I medics were instructed to classify three types of casualties in order to know which of the wounded should be treated first. Those wounded who were mortally ill were to be abandoned; those who would get well on their own should also not be treated. A third category consisted of those who might be expected to survive and recover, if they received medical treatment. Priority was thus given to treating those in this last category. My argument is against those who view the American Jewish community as mortally ill, without hope. No policy would be helpful if this were true. It is also against those who would do nothing because all is well. Rather, I argue that there is a firm basis for building a healthier and more Jewish community. The American Jewish community is that part of the triage where there are many vital signs and much to do.

The issue as I see it is therefore not one of optimism versus pessimism. I argued from the evidence about potential. I postulate robustness in terms of specific defineable dimensions of interaction and cohesion. The issue of potential relates to those aspects of community life which are a basis for building stronger and deeper roots. Simply put, it would be much more difficult to formulate policies if the level of assimilation was such that Jews did not interact extensively in economic, social, family, political, and cultural spheres or if they did not share interests and lifestyle and some common, if elusive, cultural heritage.

I argue that Jews in America constitute a community; they form networks of interaction, in part out of desire and commitment to communal survival but mostly out of interests and lifestyle. Those interactions form a strong basis of contemporary communities. But we need policies to further enhance the content of the interactions and insure that continuity has a high probability of characterizing the next generation. So we need policies to reinforce and strengthen in new ways the basis of community characteristic of the current generation of young Jewish Americans.

In part the question revolves around what comparisons are being made. Often our comparisons are between the ideal and real; between the first generation of immigrants and the fourth generation; distant from cultural roots, from an ethnic language, from foreignness, and from *Yiddishkeit*. Often we implicitly compare the nostalgia of Eastern Europe Jewry of 150 years ago to the reality of contemporary America. Yes, American Jewry is not going to die out tomorrow but is it as strong, or as flourishing, creative, and powerful as some ideal image of Jewish communal life? The answer, I suggest, relates to the comparisons we make and the costs as well as benefits of Jewish communal cohesion characteristic of the past.

The contemporary American Jewish community is strong and cohesive relative to the first and second generations where there was little basis for cohesion, where generational conflict dominated, where there were few opportunities for Jewish education and for creative religious expression, and where the rejection of cultural and religious roots was viewed as necessary for social mobility and integration. By standards that are ideal--where religious activities are central, where interaction among Jews is maximum, where Jewish knowledge is extensive, where intermarriage is zero, where Jewish culture flourishes--the contemporary American Jewish community is weak. Yet those ideals are ideals; they do not characterize any Jewish community in modern (or premodern) Jewish history. To the extent that Jewish communities were more cohesive in the past, the costs have been choice and freedom. In short, the cost to the Jewish community of modernization has been the option to choose whether and how to be Jewish. And with that choice comes the rather amazing empirical conclusion--most Jews in American society, where there is maximum choice of lifestyle and interest, where there are neither legal nor social constraints to limit religious or ethnic expressions, choose to relate to the Jewish community in a variety of ways. They are Jewish in America not in the ways in which other communities in the past were Jewish and not in all the "ideal" ways. They are Jewish by choice and thus represent the potential for enhancing Jewishness and Judaism. Hence, there are costs to ethnic-religious continuity in a free and voluntaristic society. The maximum Jewish survival associated with a Jewish political State or an imposed *Shtetl* of segregation and communal constraints involves costs as well as benefits. And of course the thrust of the argument that I made is that American Jewish communities are cohesive relative to the American context of choice and relative to the extreme end of the continuum of total assimilation.

The issue of comparison goes deeper. Do American Jews, in general, or the marginals and the intermarried in particular, have more in common with non-Jewish Americans than with orthodox segregated American Jews? That is a tough question, since American Jews have a great deal in common with American non-Jews in terms of culture and middle class modern lifestyles. Indeed, they probably have more in common in their daily lives with non-Jewish Americans of similar social class backgrounds than they have with segregated orthodox Jews whose language and lifestyles, values and attitudes are distinctive. Moreover, American Jews have much more in common with their non-Jewish neighbors than with Israeli Jews or Hasidic Jews, or Oriental Jews or with many Jewries outside of the United States. There is, of course the beautiful myth (and insistent ideology) that Jews are one--a myth perpetrated by Zionists and UJA leaders. It is based on generalization and stereotype and ironically associated as well with arch-evil Hamans and antisemites. There are powerful threads linking Jews everywhere but even more grounds for differentiation. American Jews are very much "American", as other Jewries are and have been part of their culture and society.

Thus, as long as there is an American Jewish community, and the quantitative and qualitative evidence suggests that it is going to be around for a long time, not only as a remnant but as a community of social, economic, political, and cultural centrality within world Jewry, there are ways that it can be strengthened and improved. This is where the policies fit in. These policies need to be understood in the context of the broader society within which the American Jewish community operates. Policies are there not to reinforce the status quo but to change it. The extent of change needs to take into account the constraints and freedoms characteristic of American society. The policies need to be realistic as well. For example, one could argue for the establishment of new segregated ghettos in America--no more interaction with non-Jews, no more attendance at public schools and universities, no more jobs in non-Jewish firms, etc. This policy, if implemented, would have the effect of maximizing Jewish cohesion, reducing intermarriage, and increasing Jewish awareness--knowledge and commitment. This "desired" effect is an absurd basis for policy not only because it is unrealistic in the voluntary community of American Jewry but also because there are major social and political costs associated with such a proposal.

The issue of networks, lifestyles, commonalities, linkages and ties is not just sociological jargon. The data show clearly the extensive bonds Jews have developed with each other; hence American Jewry is not a wasteland. We need to build the inner social and cultural dynamics by the development of creative policies and programs. But we need to develop these policies within the context of American Jewish communities in all their variation and their rich potential. Thus, the issue fundamental to the basis for developing policy is an assessment of, first, where we are; not only where we ought to be; not policy in a vacuum but in a context. The celebration of the strong roots of American Jewish life and the firm foundations of American Jewish continuity is not an argument that all is well and cannot be improved. To the contrary: It means that the perspective of America as a dying Jewish community with no creative future and a quality of Jewish life that diminishes from generation to generation implies one set of policies; a strong Jewish community with a firm basis for growth and a potential for the development of new forms of Jewish expression--religious and ethnic--implies other kinds of policies. The evidence available seems to me to point clearly in the direction of the latter assessment and directs us unequivocally toward creative policies to enhance Jewish cohesion, not to save a dying community. The argument against complacency is therefore not intended as a statement of *Chutzpah* for those striving for quality but a proposition of challenge and potential for creative policies.

Intermarriage and Fertility

One of the areas where issues of quality and quantity merge
and are most central to the concerns of the community and its
leadership is intermarriage. It is here where generational change
and continuity are challenged most dramatically. In no area are
more questions raised about evidence and the quality of the data.
There are indeed serious problems with the data available and
major limitations to all the studies that have been carried out. In
my review, I did not distinguish among the various types of
intermarriage and I was much too vague about the definition of
intermarriage. However, this reflects, in part, limitations of the
data and of common usage in which even marriages between a
born-Jew and a converted Jew are normally called
"intermarriages". Distinctions among intermarriage types are
critical, and need to be sharpened to make sense out of the
findings I summarized and reviewed. In particular, there is a
need to specify the differences between intermarriages which
involve conversions to Judaism (of different kinds--orthodox,
conservative, and reform) from those where there is no formal
religious conversion. There are informal ways in which the non-
Jewish born partner can identify with the Jewish community and
patterns of Jewish identification of the Jewish-born partner even
when formal conversion of the non-Jewish partner does not occur.
Jewish communal identification does not necessarily involve a
religious component.

In turn, the long term effects of intermarriage on issues of
Jewish continuity vary with the type of intermarriage. The
greater the Jewish commitment of the couple, the higher the
probability that the intermarried couple will continue to identify as
Jews and contribute to the growth, vitality, and strength of the
Jewish community. Although we have little systematic, reliable
data on this issue, it is likely that those who have formally
converted to Judaism have higher levels of Jewish commitments
than those who identify themselves as Jews but have not
converted formally. It is likely that the continuum is not perfectly
smooth and that there are other factors at the individual, family,
and community levels that affect the subsequent identification
patterns of the intermarried. Nevertheless, the evidence suggests
that we cannot simply write off the intermarried as a loss to the

Jewish community, nor can we assume that the intermarried symbolize the continuous decline of Jewish quality in America. But we need to know more, more about how the Jewishness of the intermarried (as well as the non-intermarried) changes over the life cycle, and about the longer term questions of subsequent identity and Jewishness of the couple and their children and the connections to the broader Jewish community. And we need to know how these processes are influenced by how the intermarried couple and their children are accepted by the Jewish community.

The issue of the cost of intermarriage needs to be raised more clearly and more broadly. I raised the question regarding the demographic costs of intermarriage to Jewish American fertility and population growth and to individual level measures of the quality of Jewish life characteristics of the intermarried and their families. But there is a more general communal cost that needs to be assessed. The religious divisions within the community are exacerbated by issues related to intermarriage. These divisions are already there, derived from other sources, but intermarriage and conversion, along with marriage and divorce, tend to bring these underlying divisions to the surface. This is particularly the case since these transitions involve religious institutions. The potential division and polarization is a real concern and creative policies need to focus on the ways to relate to issues of intermarriage without polarizing the Jewish community.

A related point raised is whether the intermarried are as Jewishly involved as I suggested. If indeed the intermarried are part of the Jewish community and are increasingly accepted in growing numbers and integrated, why do I treat them as part of the marginals? The response is that the attachments of some of the intermarried, particularly those who have not been formally converted to Judaism, is frequently weak. Indeed, while many (and what proportion is not known exactly) are part of the ongoing Jewish community, many of the intermarried are not well integrated and are not part of the Jewish community. It is to those more marginal segments that we need to develop creative policies. Saying *kaddish* appears to be the least effective solution to the challenges associated with finding ways to incorporate the intermarried into the Jewish community. One can be Jewish and still remain marginal on some of the dimensions of Jewish life. This is no less true for the intermarried than for the intramarried. Hence, I do not see any basis for some to argue that intermarriage is a net loss and I do not agree that it is misleading to suggest

151

that intermarriage may be a quantitative and qualitative gain for the Jewish community. There is a need to focus on the inner core of Jews and develop policies and programs to enrich that segment; at the same time policies directed to the core are unlikely to reach substantial portions of American Jewry who are on the margins, including some of the intermarried.

Some have reraised the fertility policy question, arguing that low fertility and in turn declining population growth remain critical issues for the Jewish community. Some have asserted that there is a need to "create an ideological imperative for larger families" and a "moral persuasion" for higher fertility. I do not see any evidence to support that position nationally. (If the issue is local, then migration, rather than fertility policies need to be developed.) Here, social scientific research on general populations demonstrates that population policies do not work. Moving from two to three children is not a simple transition; and it is unlikely that moral imperatives will influence the fertility behavior of most Jewish couples. The analogy to ZPG (Zero Population Growth) is indeed instructive, but in the opposite way proposed. It was argued that if ZPG discouraged people from having children, couldn't any movement accomplish the opposite goal of increasing family size? However, most demographers agree that ZPG did not result in the decline in fertility; rather ZPG was a movement that reflected the fertility changes that were occurring in a changing America. To reverse a pattern requires that the broader societal context be changed. More importantly, as I argued in the original essay, the issue is not fertility but rather the extent of marriage. In my view, the evidence unmistakably points to the conclusion that fertility policies in the American Jewish community would be a waste of resources and would focus on the wrong issue. Do we really need a debate on the "optimum" size of the Jewish community when those debates have long been abandoned in demography and where the proper focus is on issues of quality and development? The analogy to Jewish quality and on the development of creative expressions of Jewishness and Judaism is clear.

Religion and Ethnicity

My analysis tended to downplay the religious dimension of American Jewish life and argued for the variety of ways of ethnic Jewish expression among American Jews, including but not

152

necessarily restricted to the realm of religion. However, the decline in specific forms of traditional religious expression, ritual observances, and piety does not imply the declining salience of Jewish community in modern America. It does mean change and transformation and the emergence of new forms of being Jewish.

There is some evidence, largely unsystematic, of a spiritual revitalization among selected segments of the American Jewish community. And perhaps I did not sufficiently stress the institutional role of the synagogue. Some see a great search among the young for Jewish spiritual links and therefore argue that in many ways young Jewish Americans may be less secular than in the past. The quest for meaning has, some have argued, become the guiding spirit of our age. There is a powerful suggestion that the United States lacks the constraints of religious establishment and is an environmental context conducive to religious experimentation and innovation. Judaism in America is therefore in a unique position to develop new modes of religious expressions. This situation provides an opportunity to the community to build toward a strengthening of Jewishness. Yet I am arguing that other characteristics--ethnic, social, and economic (and I should add political) also provide opportunities for strengthening Jewishness that should not be ignored. We do not yet have a balance sheet to examine either gains or losses due to religious "changes" or to know the relative impact of religious modes in the lives of American Jews. My own guess is that for most American Jews, even the more religious, secularism is a more powerful set of life values than Judaism per se.

Some have argued that policies not designed primarily to enhance the religious character of American Jewish life are not likely to succeed and endure. That is not a tested assumption. In modern societies, in America and in other places where Jews live, the religious and ethnic components of Jewishness have been differentiated. But that does not mean that they are not related. It does mean that they are not always related and, when they are, they may be related in new and unprecedented ways.

A final point about the nature of Judaism in American society was not highlighted in my analysis and should be considered. It relates to the increasing polarization among the various Judaisms in America, related in part to issues of personal status and the halachic position involved (e.g., intermarriage, conversion, who is a Jew, role of women in ritual, divorce, etc.). Religious pluralism not only characterizes American society but has characterized variants of Judaism in America. The more traditional, including segments of American orthodoxy, seem to be less tolerant of the other Judaisms, or at last seem to have become more vocal about the "legitimacy" of others by the political control exercised by the orthodox rabbinate in Israel. Their control in America rests in large part with a limited population and on selected issues. At the same time that many changes in the religion of American Jews have resulted in greater similarities among religious denominations (and there are many illustrations of changes within reform, conservative and modern orthodoxy toward homogenization), there are indications of greater polarization and division between the "segregated" orthodox and others.

Policy Criticisms

When I tried to link policy issues to my analysis of the sociology of American Jews and their communities, I began with some rather vague notions. In order to be more concrete and specific, I suggested three specific policies or programs. I tried to justify each and spell out some of the ways they might work. I did not indicate how they might be implemented and continue to avoid dealing with how these suggested policies might fit into (or might need to change) the organizational apparatus in place within the Jewish community. There are hundreds of policies and programs of all kinds that are already being tried in various communities, from outreach programs for the intermarried to Jewish educational reform, from creative community projects to linkages to Israel, from new ways to express popular Jewish culture to enhanced Jewish educational activities in community centers, and dozens more. The suggestions I made should be treated as illustrative of focused activities to support and reinforce the Jewishness of targeted groups within the community.

Even those who disagreed with some of the analysis of the American Jewish community did not find too many specific objections to the policies or programs I proposed. I am sure, however, that if I set priorities among these and between these and established programs, disagreements would be more substantial. As it is now, these proposals are not threatening and not competitive with alternative ways to distribute resources. Most of the specific criticisms were directed to the development of modern Jewish studies programs in the universities and the

154

summer program for marginal Jewish youth.

In terms of the suggestion for modern Jewish studies, some argued that there is no need, since there are already many courses in Judaica in universities in the United States. And these courses do not seem to be much of a "turn on"; more of the same is therefore unjustifiable. I did not want to argue that the inclusion of modern Jewish studies in the curriculum of universities should be justified on the grounds of the salience of modern Jewish studies to the Jewish commitments of the Jewish students. Rather, my point was that the inclusion of modern Jewish studies in the curriculum on academic and intellectual grounds may have latent, unintended consequences. The policy attempted to address an important stage of the life cycle in an intellectual academic context and indeed has largely not been carried out. I have argued against the justification of modern Jewish study courses on particularistic ethnic lines. While I do not know how many attend existing courses, the objective of the policy was to change all that.

The proposal to send marginal teenagers to a summer program in Israel was faulted for what I view as its strength--the focus on those teenagers on the margins of the Jewish community. While there is clearly much more that could be done for those teenagers who are part of the "core", I continue to feel that programs targeted to the weakest segments of the community have particular merit. Several questions were raised about the proposal to provide this summer experience free of charge. Will free activities be appreciated? How effective are programs that are free or heavily subsidized? I had considered these questions in the initial draft and I concluded that "free" would have more advantages than disadvantages. I am not prepared to overemphasize the point and the best I can hope for is for a pilot project to test out the alternatives carefully and systematically. On the other hand, a focus on the marginals of the Jewish community, however they are defined (and the definition should vary by community context) and for whatever stage of the life cycle, is critical. While I see no objection to expanding the summer program idea to the affiliated, the policy direction is toward incorporating the less affiliated within the community. Clearly policies designed for the core will rarely reach the marginals; policies designed for the marginals might reach the core.

155

The discussion of the leadership gap between Israel and American Jews, and, in particular the gender and religious differences that such a gap entails, has a number of policy implications. I did not spell these out in detail and I continue to be at a loss to know how to effectively bridge those gaps. There are bases for communication among leaders in both countries, and some shared goals, but it is also clear that these are changing. The leadership elite of Israel is being replaced by those who have less in common with the organizational and religious elite of American Jewry. I see no immediate solution beyond developing continual exchanges between America and Israel and emphasizing mutual respect for the legitimacy and contribution of both communities to the future of world Jewry. While I would prefer a greater symmetry, and reject the implications of "dependency" on both sides, I am aware of the difficulties of symmetry from both the Zionist and religious perspectives. Perhaps complementarities should be considered.

My argument that policies should be based on social scientific evidence may represent a new strategy for the American Jewish community. There is much to do and a firm foundation to build upon. Our future as a Jewish community in America is neither beyond hope nor assured. We are, however, that part of the triage where policies can affect the vigor and robustness of the future.

AFTERWORD

Sheldon M. Schreter
Director-General of The Israel-Diaspora Institute
Tel Aviv, Israel

You don't have to agree with everything Calvin Goldscheider says in his essay - and I don't - to recognize the value of what he has done. This includes, in addition to debunking the "demographic doomsday" scenario for American Jews, the reaffirmation that it is necessary and feasible to devise policies for their future, and to link policies to social science research findings.

If these points sound basic, that does not mean they don't need reinforcing in Jewish life today. The assumption that assimilation and disappearance are inevitable in the long run is very widespread and it has a pernicious, subtle, constricting effect on the perception (and therefore the living) of Jewish life in the present. Unstoppable social and cultural forces are seen to be leading our children (or theirs) further and further afield, and many subconsciously despair of our capacity to resist the unravelling and eventual sundering of the Jewish world we have known.

The various experts and interpreters of our complicated reality - the religious and political leaders, the media-people and the academics - often seem to confirm that the range of viable Jewish options is steadily dwindling, or else veering off into avenues of extreme religious and/or political expression, of limited appeal. They frequently try, to their credit, to motivate us into action to change the direction of things, and sometimes they succeed for awhile. Ultimately, for many, their well-intentioned warnings are demoralizing.

Goldscheider forcefully demonstrates that the eulogies for American Jewry are premature, to say the least. Modernization changes Jewish options and dynamics, sometimes extensively, but does not for the most part eradicate them. The research contains some indications of where and how to concentrate our initiatives in optimizing the options for Jewish life, and of what we need to know more about before reaching conclusions.

In other words, Goldscheider is saying, while social forces act to influence us, we can also act back on them and shape the Jewish alternatives of the future. We don't have to limit ourselves to reacting to crises, nor assume ourselves to be subject to anonymous social currents. We can and should - after analyzing and understanding our reality - take specific policy initiatives designed to effect desired changes.

158

The discussion of intermarriage provides a useful, if controversial example. Goldscheider emphasizes the finding that the Jewish differences between the intermarried and the non-intermarried have *narrowed* over time. While this indicates to some extent a general trend to secularization or non-affiliation among younger Jews, its more significant message is that the intermarried don't necessarily wish to stop being Jews! The community does not automatically have to sit *shiva* for them, nor regard them as lost to the Jewish people forever. A variety of approaches to re-integrating them into the community, encouraging the conversion of their non-Jewish spouses and the Jewish socialization of their children, may be adopted, with reasonable prospects of success.

The overall approach is salutary and constructive, a useful antidote to the fatigue and cynicism which are often encountered in contemporary Jewish life, and which serve as the familiar rationale for preserving the status quo from meaningful change.

Goldscheider relinquishes the safety and comfort of academic detachment by dealing with the practical applications of his knowledge. He commits himself to specific proposals and takes risks in discussing difficult issues such as intermarriage, *yerida,* the robustness (or not) of the American Jewish community, the definition of Jewish cohesion and Israel-Diaspora relations. Rather than listing my reservations on some of his remarks (all of which were raised by one or another of the commentators in this volume), I would prefer to point out that he has succeeded in sparking a real give-and-take on priorities and policies. This will hopefully be extended in the community at large, and in Jewish communities elsewhere as well. Jewish life and communal policy stand to benefit greatly from such a process.

One question to which Goldscheider and his commentators give a clear answer is: Can we manage without paranoia? Does Jewish continuity necessitate threats of one kind or another (anti-semitism, assimilation) to propel it forward? Without falling prey to complacency, I believe *all* the contributors to this volume would accept the notion that Jewish life, in order to thrive, must be based primarily on a positive, rather than a negative impetus, on what Jews share and can create together, rather than on the fear of what an unpredictable environment could do to us. This encapsulates the central challenge of Jewish life today, as mapping a positive course is always much more difficult than banding together in self-defence against external threats.

A number of basic policy issues for Jewish life are raised which clearly require further thought and development, especially when choices have to be made in allocating limited resources. Two which come to mind in particular are:

A. Should emphasis be placed more on developing programs and services for the committed, or partially committed, in order to consolidate and upgrade their involvement; or rather on outreach to the "marginals", with a view to integrating them into the circle of communal activity?

B. Should emphasis be placed on developing policies tailored specifically for local needs for implementation at the local community (or federation) level; or rather on broad, national policy, which will provide an overall sense of direction and purpose, and which different communities will then adapt to one extent or another? What is the optimum combination between the two?

The specific issues raised in the course of Goldscheider's essay and dialogue with his commentators are numerous, and could readily serve as the beginning of a policy research agenda for American Jewry. For that reason, it may be worth summarizing them briefly, as an indication of where future, policy-oriented research efforts could usefully be applied:

1. *Jewish Women* - What are the changes which have occurred among American Jewish women - educationally, occupationally, economically, socially, religiously, culturally, etc. - over the last 30 years? What are the continuities? How does this affect their participation in Jewish life, in women's and in general communal organizations? How does it influence their participation in Israel-Diaspora relations, with regard to Israeli women, with regard to women's issues in Israel, etc.?

2. *Yordim* - What are their social characteristics, needs, attitudes to the Jewish community and to Israel? How can they be integrated into the Jewish community?

160

3. *Israel Programs* - What is their impact on participants, short- and long-term? How should follow-up on program participants be handled, so as to optimize this impact? How much of a difference does a peer interaction component in an Israel program make, in terms of impact on participants?

4. *Intermarriage* - What are the characteristics, general and Jewish, of those who do intermarry and those who do not? Are there significant differences between the various types of intermarriages (Jewish male and non-Jewish female and vice-versa, marriages where the non-Jewish partner does and does not convert)? What are the long-term patterns of involvement/non-involvement of the couple and their children in the Jewish community, and to what causal factors can these be attributed?[2] Which policies would serve best to integrate them into the community?

5. *Changes in Leadership Elites* - What are the shifts in occupation, education, Jewish and general values, Jewish identity, attitude to Israel, attitudes toward intermarriage, etc., among younger American Jewish leadership circles, as compared to older ones?

6. *Jewish Studies Programs on University Campuses* - What are their latent functions for Jewish reinforcement, for individual students, for Jewish life on campus? What, if any, are their "spillover" effects for the Jewish community adjacent to the campus, e.g., in terms of adult Jewish education, participation of lecturers and students in communal institutions, etc.? To what extent are there contradictions between academic and

----

[2] One wag contended that the children of intermarriages were highly likely to marry Jews, since their Jewish-born parent was probably favorable or at least neutral, while their non-Jewish-born parent was strongly in favor since that is exactly what he/she had done! While this point is hardly serious, the marriage and other demographic patterns of the children of intermarriages are surely an important topic for research.

communal concerns?

7. *Jewish Students* - Have their numbers, attitudes, priorities and Jewish concerns changed or remained stable over the last 10-15 years? What factors influence the extent of their involvement with official campus Jewish organizations (e.g., Hillel), informal Jewish social networks, the local Jewish community? What role is played/could be played by Jewish fraternities and sororities? How do they relate to Jewish holidays spent for the first time(s) outside the family unit?

8. *Occupational Networks* - How do these actually function? What Jewish reinforcement is derived by the high concentration of Jews in specific professions, e.g., law and medicine? What policies could mobilize such occupational networks creatively on behalf of Jewish communal concerns?

9. *Jewish Residential Patterns* - To what extent are high-density Jewish neighborhoods essential to the maintenance of Jewish institutions and communal life? To what extent do Jewish families take proximity to Jewish facilities into account in making residential choices, and which factors best explain their inclination to do so? What are the current trends in Jewish residential concentration/dispersion?

10. *Community Demographic/Sociological Studies* - What are the demographic trends in specific communities, measured at regular intervals (e.g., every five years)? What are the demographic trends across communities (assuming some standardization of studies for the sake of comparability)? What are emergent trends in marriage childbearing, divorce, migration, etc.?

11. *Budgetary Studies* - What is the implementation cost of various policy ideas, e.g., providing free Jewish education for all children from the third on, or sending "marginal" teenagers for a free, one-month program in Israel? If we could develop an index of the extent to which a given communal program facilitates interaction among Jews (Goldscheider's operational measure of communal cohesion), what is the comparative cost of

one (analytical) unit of interaction for different programs? Can such an exercise help in establishing priorities among different programs?

12. *Jewish Religious Pluralism* - Is the pattern of cooperation among the different religious streams within American Judaism in danger of breaking down, as a process of polarization gradually drives them further apart and erodes the basis for common action? Are the tensions surrounding religion-state relations in Israel a negative input into this situation? What social factors explain what appears to be a decline in the vigor and influence of moderate orthodoxy over the past 10-20 years? Is there any serious likelihood of working out joint procedures on divorce and conversion, so as to avert divisiveness and schism? Has a religious schism already occurred, *de facto?*

13. *Specific Jewish Sub-Groups* - What are the Jewish characteristics and program needs of Jewish singles, single-parent families, widows/widowers, etc.?

This list could easily be expanded. Additional questions have a place on the policy research agenda, e.g., who makes and implements policy in the Jewish community; how to assess the effectiveness - and the latent functions - of Jewish education; how to encourage and nurture religious/spiritual creativity within the community; how to cope with the changes in what many Jews regard as normatively Jewish, and where to draw the line between adaptation and continuity. The point here was not to present a final list, but simply to illustrate the range of relevant issues touched upon and clarified by Goldscheider and his commentators.

I will conclude these remarks with a few personal acknowledgements. I wish to thank one of the Israel-Diaspora Institute's founders and long-time supporters, Mr. Jack Cummings of Montreal, Canada, whose generosity made possible our implementation of this project. I want to thank the twelve commentators, all extremely busy people, who took the time to read and critique the original essay, and to prepare their remarks in writing for this volume.

Most of all, I wish to thank Professor Calvin Goldscheider, for agreeing to accept the central role in this process, and for carrying it through so well. His admirable synthesis of scholarship and Jewish commitment set a standard well worthy of emulation.

I sincerely hope that this exercise in joint policy deliberation provokes and deepens the thinking about these issues in the community at large, and leads thereby to better policies with better results. That was the objective of the Israel-Diaspora Institute in sponsoring this project, and one of the main purposes for which it was created.

CONTRIBUTORS

Calvin GOLDSCHEIDER is Professor of Judaic Studies and Sociology at Brown University and was formerly Professor of Demography and Sociology at the Hebrew University. In recent years his research has focused on the sociological and demographic aspects of ethnicity in Israel and in the United States, with particular emphasis on comparative and historical issues associated with Jews and their communities. He has published extensively in these areas and is the author of several major books and monographs that present the detailed evidence underlying the essay in this volume. Two recent books, *The Transformation of the Jews* (University of Chicago Press, 1984) co-authored with Alan Zuckerman and *Jewish Continuity and Change: Emerging Patterns in America* (Indiana University Press, 1986), examine systematically the impact of modernization on the assimilation of the Jews in Europe, the United States, and Israel.

Reuven HAMMER is the Dean and Assistant Professor of Rabbinic Literature at the Jewish Theological Seminary in Jerusalem. He served previously as a congregational rabbi in the United States, and has published two books and numerous articles on Jewish scholarly and educational issues.

Rita E. HAUSER is an international lawyer and Senior Partner in the Wall Street firm of Stroock & Stroock & Lavan. She is the Chair of the National Executive Committee of the American Jewish Committee and is the former United States representative

165

to the United Nations Commission on Human Rights.

Harold HIMMELFARB is an Associate Professor of Sociology at the Ohio State University in Columbus. He has written widely on American Jewish identification and Jewish education and is the immediate Past President of the Association for the Sociological Study of Jewry.

Richard G. HIRSCH is Executive Director of the World Union for Progressive Judaism, based in Jerusalem. He represents the Reform Movement in executive bodies of the Jewish Agency and the World Zionist Organization, and lectures in Social Ethics at Hebrew Union College. He writes frequently in various publications and has authored four books on the application of Judaism to current social issues.

Wolfe KELMAN has served for 35 years as Executive Vice-President of the Rabbinical Assembly. He is an Adjunct Assistant Professor of History at the Jewish Theological Seminary in New York, and is recognized as one of the central figures in the Conservative Movement. He has a broad array of organizational positions (American and international), professional positions and publications.

Deborah Dash MOORE is Chair of the Department of Religion and Associate Professor of Jewish Studies at Vassar College. She has published two books and numerous articles and reviews, primarily on American Jewish history.

Bernard REISMAN is Professor of American Jewish Communal Studies and Director of the Hornstein Program in Jewish Communal Service at Brandeis University. He writes and lectures on issues pertaining to the American Jewish community and its organizational structures.

Jonathan SARNA is Associate Professor of American Jewish History and Academic Director of the Center for the Study of the American Jewish Experience at the Hebrew Union College -

Jewish Institute of Religion in Cincinnati. He has written or edited five books and numerous articles and reviews on American Jewish History.

Alexander M. SCHINDLER is President of the Union of American Hebrew Congregations, the synagogue movement of Reform Judaism in the United States and Canada. Recognized as one of the senior spokesmen of American Jewry as a whole, he served as Chairman of the Conference of Presidents of the Major American Jewish Organizations during the first years of Menahem Begin's tenure as Prime Minister of Israel.

Charles E. SILBERMAN is an author who has written extensively on American society, education, automation and other issues. His most recent book, *A Certain People: American Jews and their Lives Today* (New York: Summit Books, 1985) is of direct relevance to the subject of this volume, and has attracted considerable attention and comment.

Ira SILVERMAN was President of the Reconstructionist Rabbinical College in Philadelphia at the time he wrote his comments for this collection. He has recently become Executive Director of the 92nd Street "Y", a unique Jewish cultural and recreational institution in New York City. His previous experience included directing the Institute for Jewish Policy Planning and Research of the Synagogue Council of America.

Jacob B. UKELES is an independent planning and management consultant. Between 1981 and 1985, he served as Executive Director for Community Services at the New York Federation of Jewish Philanthropies. He worked previously in various planning positions in Hartford and New York, has lectured on this subject at several universities and has authored various articles on both general and Jewish public management and planning.

167